Behind the Pictures

Dear Shana,

It was a pleasure to connect with you again. This is just one more perspective on autism.

Enjoy.

E—

Related books of interest

The Girl Who Spoke With Pictures
Autism Through Art
Eileen Miller
Foreword by Robert Nickel, M.D.
Illustrated by Kim Miller

Apples for Cheyenne
Autism, Fun and Friendship
Elizabeth Gerlach
Illustrated by Kim Miller

STRATEGIES FOR CHANGE

Behind the Pictures

EILEEN MILLER

Foreword by Nehama Baum, Ph.D. C. Psych

Library of Congress Cataloging in Publication Data

Miller, Eileen, 1962-
  Behind the Pictures : Strategies for Change / Eileen Miller ; foreword by Nehama Baum.

ISBN 978-0-9835141-0-7

Companion book to *The Girl Who Spoke With Pictures*, 2008

Operation Just One More…
so just one more can understand

ACKNOWLEDGEMENTS

I would like to thank my husband for his long standing patience and support. You are the love of my life!

Many thanks to my two very different and lovely daughters who have given me the greatest experience of my life.

I want to especially thank Tricia Pinkerton for her valuable final editing and advice.

I would like to express my appreciation to Nehama Baum for taking the time out of her busy schedule to write the foreword.

Thank you to the MukiBaum Treatment Centers for extending their friendship and cooperation in granting me permission for using excerpts from the "Come to Your Senses Conference 2009" book.

A special thanks to Kirk Grow for our chats in the morning and for helping me to tap into those memories, the poignant emotions of years passed.

I would like to acknowledge the wonderful Douglas County Early Intervention team, many who are retired by now. They were my mentors and great friends.

Finally, to my Lord who has taught me so much in this rich life. To Him be all the credit and the glory.

CONTENTS

FOREWORD

When a child is born, a couple's life changes forever. The focus in the family shifts from the "Us" to the child. Naturally, it is a time of happiness and also of stress. Answering the needs of the new born means being constantly attentive and in the child's service. Being a mother (and a father) to a child with a disability, regardless of the specific diagnosis of the child, creates a whole new world of additional unexpected challenges the family did not plan and was not prepared for.

Muki, our son was born with cerebral palsy and deafness. When the doctor gave us the diagnosis of CP he also added "put him in an institution because he will be a piece of meat you will carry all your life," and at that moment our lives changed.

Our dream child was no more. And our journey to give our child whatever he needed started. We had to let go of the "Dream Child" and allow our son, Muki to Become.

CP is a visible disability and maybe easier to recognize. Autism is usually invisible and harder to diagnose. Parents many times will say to professionals "Something is wrong with my child" only to hear "do not worry, he or she will grow out of it" and the parent is left with a sense of anxiety knowing that something is not right, feeling the urgency that something has to be done… NOW… and not knowing what.

The agony of hearing: "Autism!" The dream child that is "no more". In this process of knowing the family faces the essential need to allow the autistic child to be re-born as a real child with all the challenges of *"not knowing how life will be"* that are associated with that. Facing the burden of autism is very hard and all-encompassing as expressed by one mother "I would give anything to hear one word, to have him point to anything, to something". But it never happens and I am left with this feeling of nothingness.

For many years we were a specialized foster home to many children with complex disabilities among them a couple of children with autism. Learning about autism is but a fraction of one aspect of what autism is. Living it day in and day out is a learning process of an experiential way. This type of knowledge does not stay isolated in your head. It is a visceral knowledge obtained through life.

For ten years we have fostered a girl that came to us when she was nine years old. One night I "learned" and really understood what autism is. I can still visualize the situation and feel it in my heart. I put Lola (not her real name) to bed. Lola, who was non-verbal, was standing on the bed while I was putting her pajamas on. She was just standing there. She did not resist. She did not cooperate. She was just standing there. After she was dressed I asked her for a hug. There was no response. She did not motion an agreement or disagreement. She was just standing there. I hugged her and she was just standing there. I felt that I was holding a non-existent body in my arms. There was no child there, only an empty body. And I knew then the desperation of a mother. I knew then what autism was.

A few years ago I read a book titled *The Girl who Spoke with Pictures*. I was struck by the beauty of Kim's paintings and by her talent. Working with people with autism and helping develop their artistic talent the paintings spoke to me about Ability and confirmed my belief that there is someone there even though it might look completely blank. As well, the paintings spoke to me about hope--, hope for the child and hope for the parents. Hope that if I, mother or father, will learn how to reach my child, not give up and keep searching for that key that will enable contact maybe in forms other than what I wanted. Eileen's words in the book illustrated the paintings and gave a voice to Kim through her paintings. That is how I met Eileen Miller the author of the book and Kim's mother and advocate. I was struck by Kim's story and by Eileen's wisdom, resolve and persistence to continue and find solutions that will help Kim. While trying to figure out what to do Eileen also went through a self-exploration of who she was and who her daughter was.

I was so impressed with the book that I made contact with Eileen and invited both her and Kim to attend our 3rd 2009 Come to Your Senses International conference. I also asked her if she would be willing to present and share with the audience her journey as Kim's mother, her experiences, her feelings and what she had learned through this journey

Eileen's presentation touched many people in the audience including other parents to children with disabilities many with autism.

Eileen's presentation and her wonderful way of sharing and explaining her journey and what she has learned during it solidified my appreciation of her.

I was very honored when Eileen asked me to write the Foreword for her second book *Behind the Pictures: Strategies for Change*.

As its name reflects in this book, through the story of hers and Kim's journeys Eileen Miller provide some answers to the "…and now what?" and how do I /we do it?

She says: "In my opinion, the treatment for autism should start with the family." Since *"If Mama ain't happy, Ain't nobody happy"*. And so, Eileen, based on her personal journey wrote a book that attempts to provide parents with a roadmap for the "How to do it".

The names of each chapter in the book reflect not only the story of the journey but also give a hint of some of the challenges, strategies and solutions that Eileen developed through her own and her family experiences.

Through Shards of Glass expresses the sense of a life that was ruined, fragmented and turned to pieces by the existential demands of a child with such complex manifestations of her autism. Already here, at this early stage of the journey, through her struggle Eileen finds out that maybe, if she lets go a bit of her desperate wishes for her child to function and be somewhat like the other kids she encounters in the school, some rebuilding can occur. She listens to the wise words of the teacher and learns to reduce somewhat the intensity of the "push". However, Eileen, like other parents was still impacted by the reality of hers and Kim's challenges. Worries like; "What is Kim doing? What should she be doing? How do we get her there?" are part of the life of every parent to a child with such unpredictable and predictable unique expressions of the child. The story about Kim running away as a 3½ year old and the frantic search for her is a good manifestation of the above and the realization a parent needs to find regarding life compromises that needed to be accepted. For Eileen, at that moment, was the realization that she needed to find a "mother's helper," that she needed to have another pair of eyes to help her provide her daughter with what she needed and at the same time, enable her to fulfill her other functions of a wife, mother to her other daughter and her own self.

The chapter *Reclaiming Life* focuses on a few aspects of life that are often compromised by parents. It speaks about sleep deprivation, environment safety and furnishing the house. The chapter provides advice for self-care strategies that, according to Eileen, parents must practice. The chapter further speaks about the experience of Depression and Grief that are associated with a denial of these essential self-care aspects and might be the result of such denial.

The next chapter focuses through *Journal Examples* on some powerful strategies to achieve change. This is expanded in the following chapter titled *Mind and Body Connection* in which she emphasizes how we, parents and care givers need to learn to interpret the "body" language of the child. Like Kim's paintings that Eileen understood to be Kim's language of communication, body expressions and behavior are a language of communication too.

So, how can we do it? What do we need to do in order to not only find solutions and figure out what our child needs are, but also how we can become the best and most powerful advocates for our child and maybe through that, propel change for other children too.

So many years ago, when Muki was 2½ years old children were not accepted to school until they became 5 years old. I went to the school for children with CP to be rejected because of that regulation. I specialized in CP before Muki was born and I knew that in CP, just like in autism, the younger the intervention the better the chances for growth and development. So I fought, I advocated, I knocked on every door I found and eventually I succeeded to convince the school board and the regulation was changed. Muki started school when he was young, and as a result other children we also able to start school at an age of 2 to 3.

In *Build Support* Eileen provides not only a roadmap of the path parents need to take in order to succeed in achieving their goals. She also provides the strategies needed for such success. She mentions that this involves addressing first the parents and explaining to them what they need to commit to in building supports for their kids. It continues with a part addressing professionals explaining to them and to parents, the need of coming together and teaming in partnership. Towards the establishment of such a partnership the parents, on the other hand, needs to struggle with fears and issues such as "how can we as parents let go of our kid? How can we trust care givers that they will do as well as we do? How can we acknowledge that teachers and aids might know as much, if not more than we know? And finally learn how to acknowledge our own knowledge of our child and their challenges.

From being a parent and learning to let Kim Be and from getting to a point of acceptance of the "newly born" Kim, Eileen became a teacher and a support system to other parents. Parents need a supporting hand, someone that will understand, will know what that is all about and Eileen provides that. Touching on questions such as Eileen explains "How does one reclaim life? How can a parent go through the grief about the lost dream child? And how can a parent learn to live and take care of him/herself.

The book, in addition to providing strategies, gives also some "how to" tricks so that parents would not need to through as much trial and error in a process of figuring out the "how to". Recipes such as: "I would suggest a 'sound machine' to mask ambient noise in the house and the neighborhood. Kim, like some individuals with autism, has a hypersensitive hearing and hears noises a block away." Such recipes might save others from the example of a reality of "unfortunately, we did not understand autism at the time and we mistakenly put the fan in our room to mask her screaming".

In conclusion I feel that Eileen gives an outline of a clear and detailed roadmap weaved with stories of her own experience of HOW to think about all these challenges and how to create the specific unique solution for each situation. Her motto is: *"Give a man a fish, you feed him for a day, you teach a man to fish, you feed him for a life time" –(Chinese Proverb)* Eileen, in this book, gives us universal examples that can touch each parent's heart and in that we can experience that "we are all in it together".

Nehama Baum, Ph.D., C. Psych
MukiBaum Treatment Centres
Toronto, Ontario, Canada
March 2011

INTRODUCTION

During the course of writing the original manuscript for *The Girl Who Spoke With Pictures*, my focus changed. In reality, the work evolved into two separate books. The manuscript was at one time in perfect chronological order, however, the stories had greater impact when condensed into subjects rather than as they happened. In many instances months or even years passed between the observation and discovery, so the significance of the lesson learned was lost. Since one portion of the text dealt with the interpretation of autism through my daughter, Kim Miller's, artwork, it only made sense divide the manuscript into separate books. By examining how she processed information and the impressions she had about the world around her, we gained a vast amount of knowledge about communication of one autistic individual. The other section of the manuscript was dedicated to personal stories of how we began to critically think about creative problem solving. We were pushing toward solutions for the ever changing, complicated challenges of parenting a child with autism. Autism is a multifaceted condition that requires significant consideration before developing a plan of action on the point of where to begin.

After connecting with numerous people around the world on social networking sites, such as Facebook and Twitter, I am struck by the private stories of parents who are struggling with the same issues and challenges that I faced over 20 years ago. Even though my daughter's artwork carved out a path, an avenue of communication of her own, there was still much to be learned regarding her ever challenging symptoms of autism. However each issue and each resolution was only one key that opened only one door to a hallway in the palace of her mind. There were many more keys, and I didn't possess them. Rather, they were found in the plans for modifications, in the environment, and in the people *Behind the Pictures.*

This book is for those parents who are still trying to find the keys to their children, who are still searching for help in daily living, who want practical strategies that any average, sleep deprived, overwhelmed person can use to make positive steps towards change. It is for them that I am writing about the process of critical thinking and problem solving through my personal stories.

<u>CHAPTER 1</u>

Through Shards of Glass

I have always told people that I would crawl a mile through crushed glass for one word of hope or encouragement. Not that I intend to be dramatic, but there was very little to be positive about when the word autism was spoken. The year was 1991. The scant few everyday articles that a housewife could get her hands on, spoke dismally about those affected by the condition. Titles with words whispering doom such as "unreachable" and "nightmare," accompanied by pictures of children rocking in a corner or curled in a fetal position shot a piercing agony straight to my heart.

Those images and the heaviness in my heart contrasted greatly with the playroom that I saw at the local Early Intervention (EI) Center. It was brightly lit, with cheery colors painted on the walls and play stations for the children like any ordinary preschool room. I don't know exactly what I was expecting, but with serious words like; "disability," "special needs," and "autism," the scene seemed incongruous. Here was where it all started and it was here that I continually returned in my mind's eye; reviewing my tape of memories, sieving through the scattered disjointed segments for words of wisdom and hope. Kim, my youngest daughter, was barely 3 years old when she was diagnosed with classic autism. Months of hard work were spent in this classroom before she received the official label for symptoms that perplexed me. The future artist had not yet begun her journey. Her Rosetta stone lay undiscovered and still buried underneath the many symptoms of her condition. The ability to reveal what she was thinking in her art, and her desire to communicate what she wanted to say by using various concrete mediums, was still years away from the significant step toward overcoming the many difficulties of her autism.

I stood at the door, our first day in the Early Intervention room, with 2½ year old Kim straddled across my hip, poised to enter. Carrying my toe headed "wild child" was the fastest way, the only way to get her into the building and into the classroom without bringing on a tantrum. What lay beyond the door would either be the answer to our prayers or a long road leading to a dead end. She gripped me like Koala bear and hid her head in the hollow of my neck, like she had so many times before. We were both terrified but for different reasons; Kim, because of the unknown environment and me for the fact that the truth of how we really lived might be revealed. I almost turned around to retreat to the relative safety of my car and subsequently home, but suddenly the door opened. The thought of our situation not improving was more compelling than any fear I felt. We made a dramatic entrance as I stepped through the threshold. Kim threw her head back with full force, arching her back, screeching at the top of her lungs. I had become accustomed to her impulsive outbursts and instinctively reached out my hand to catch her head. Staggering slightly as she knocked my 5 foot 2 inch frame off balance, I put her down to explore the exciting child friendly room. The teacher, Janet, approached me as I regained my composure to introduce the other members of the class and their mothers. I was flustered and embarrassed about the outburst we made on our entry into the room, but Janet didn't seem to notice.

It was always difficult anytime we were away from home to focus on the discussion at hand, for the fact that my eyes were always on Kim. Without child proof locks and latches, she just pulled out drawers filled with toys, opened cupboard doors, running from one thing to the next. I constantly followed behind her either restoring the drawers to their prior state or heading off her intentions before she could disturb any of the contents within. This was no time to engage in chit chat. After class settled down, for "circle time," where the little children sang songs adding sign language with their hands, Kim continued to wander around the room. I tried to herd her towards the group of children until Janet invited me to sit down. My eyes were on my daughter the whole time because she could not seem to join us. Subsequent classes continued on in the same manner for over a month, with me chasing my hyperactive child, restoring what she had disturbed and guarding the door so that "Houdini" would not escape. She had not followed one direction, took no notice of her peers, did not play with toys as they were designed and did not join in any organized activity. I was miserable because it appeared as though she was not learning anything. The group would be quietly working then suddenly, the silence would be broken by a screech of a tantrum, the noise of us grappling and wrestling.

At one point during the class time, an assistant would come take the children to a play center in the basement to have unstructured play time. It always panicked me when someone else was watching my daughter. Experience told me that she would either escape, eat or do something inappropriate, but after reassurances from the staff, I reluctantly let her go. I cemented my body to the chair in the office although in my mind, I was tense as a spring.

I was reassured by all of the staff that these were trained assistants who had experience handling even the most challenging behavior. I would have to admit to myself that they were far more equipped with knowledge and experience deal with Kim than I was up to this point. All of the parents followed the teacher into her office to talk about goals for our children, our family values, and other concerns. It was also a time for the parents to ask the teacher questions about concerns regarding treatments their children were receiving and talk about issues they experienced during the week. We were all encouraged to summarize briefly challenges our children had. Some of the therapies for these toddlers involved physical therapy, occupational therapy and speech therapy as well. All of the children seemed to have labels for the symptoms that affected them. When it came my time to share, I had a difficult time putting the struggles that we experienced into words. The symptoms that I described sounded more like behavioral problems or complaints of an undisciplined child.

It wasn't as though Kim was my first experience at raising a child. I often received compliments from total strangers when we were out in the community. Marcia, my oldest daughter who was 2 years older than Kim, was a very active, precocious child in her own right. People stopped me to tell me how skilled that I was as a parent. I was fairly confident of my ability to be a good mother, so why was managing my youngest child's behavior so difficult and different? First of all, Marcia had receptive language even before she could verbalize, she seemed to take in what I was saying. She also bonded emotionally to me, caring whether I left the room or not, and was attentive to the people in her immediate area.

My confidence in being able to parent a child with special needs was at an extremely low ebb. At first, I didn't know why I needed to be at the Early Intervention Center. After all, they were the professionals; they already knew the how to treat someone with autism. I was hoping that I could drop Kim off at class and a couple of hours later, after they worked with her and fixed her, I would pick her up. Of course that would take weeks but I would be patient after all, it was Kim who had the problem. There must be quick fix pill, procedure, or therapy that we could apply and get on with our lives together. I was frustrated that Kim did not get a referral to go see a physician, although there was not anything physically wrong with her body.

Perhaps, my part was just to approve of the plan, I attended numerous meetings, but then they would take it from there.

One particular day was extremely stressful. I was trying to assist my daughter in a task by touching her and she would have nothing of it. On this morning, Kim and I were in one of our physical struggles. I was trying to get her to attend to a craft project that required painting. I dipped the paintbrush into the cup and handed it to Kim, who took it and then decided to throw a tantrum on the floor. Wildly, she jerked the paint brush, spattering paint all over me and the carpet and just barely missing the seat of a nearby aide's pants. By that time, the other parents had gotten used to our grappling and paid little attention to us. Instead, they were intent on working with their children on the project before them.

There was a lot of noise as Kim screeched and the other parents raised their voices over the din continuing to giving their children guidance and instructions, and all of a sudden, Janet raised her voice and said, "Everyone be quiet!"

The room went totally silent. I was embarrassed once more because my daughter and I were disrupting class. The teacher turned her attention towards us and instructed me to show Kim how to paint. Her hands were practically shaking, her strokes so deliberate. Loudly and enthusiastically in the moment of surprise, I said "Good girl!" Kim postured her hands and started to screech. Janet very quietly told me to speak to her in a low, monotone voice. Janet had needed the time to observe our interactions in order to distinguish what would and would not work for Kim and me. She recognized that Kim was on sensory overload and that my ordinarily appropriate responses were just too stimulating in that already over-stimulated environment. Once again, Kim was able to take a few more swipes of paint on her project before she was distracted by other things. Racked by disappointment, I retreated to sit on a soft cushion at the opposite side of the room to put my head in my hands. As I watched Kim wander around the room aimlessly like a ghost, Janet came over. She sat beside me on the cushion and asked where Kim was now. I carelessly flung my hand out in her direction. As Janet caught my gaze with hers she spoke gently, "Ask yourself: 'Where do I want Kim to be?'" My eyes welling up with tears, I told her that I just wanted her to do what everyone else was doing at the time. I wanted her to be able to participate in an activity like the other children and mothers were doing. Janet said softly, "Then consider: 'How do I get her there?'"

In hindsight I should have been extremely grateful for giving me one of the most fundamental strategies for change, but I couldn't recognize the value of that piece of advice wrapped up in kind words. I was so filled with hurt emotion and bruised ego that it took a few years for me to learn to apply this philosophy of:

"Where is Kim now? Where do you want her to be?" and "How do we get her there?"

What Janet in essence was doing, was to bring to a halt the chain reaction of events. She was circumventing my habit of bodily struggling with Kim, which always triggered a negative reaction and in turn caused me to withdraw. She turned my thinking around from forcing Kim physically to do what I wished, to building a structure of support to *guide* to where I wanted her to be and *refine* her focus. Janet was telling me to envision the goal, determine how far Kim was from that mark and then devise a plan on how to move her forward closer to that target. It would have been so simple for her to have instructed me on how to handle each and every situation as they came up, but more importantly, she was teaching me how to use a problem solving strategy, a formula that would serve me far beyond the time that I spent in that Early Intervention classroom.

"Give a man a fish, you feed him for a day,
you teach a man to fish, you feed him for a lifetime."

~Chinese Proverb

CHAPTER 2

If Mama Ain't Happy...

One of the most daunting issues of dealing with autism is the lag time between the child exhibiting symptoms and the point of diagnosis. This is especially difficult for the parents like me, whose child is born exhibiting symptoms of autism. Even though the education, training and awareness of professionals as well as the general public has done much to demystify the condition. The period of time from birth to diagnosis is enough to strain relationships of even the healthiest of families. By the time diagnosis occurs, family relationships are so compressed and constricted that the damage has already been done.

The next two chapters will be dedicated to the examination of the deconstruction of the family unit by way my own personal stories, analyzing the problems, and then finally discussing possible solutions in once again restoring family structure. The place to begin treating autism is in the basic family structure. This is the primary environment and the root for managing behavior. It is imperative to create a functional family atmosphere.

Our story:

As I have previously stated, parenting my first child came naturally to me. I felt comfortable with my skills as disciplinarian, educator, and nurturer. Everything I had learned up to this point gave me more confidence everyday. When Kim was born all the rules or formulas for successful guidance in my repertoire had to be thrown out, tossed out, they just didn't apply.

Kim was born in the early hours of a rainy spring afternoon in 1988. I was much more tired than after my previous delivery two years before. I had heard that every birth is unique, just as individual as the children who are born, but something was different, although both labors were unusually short.

This one had been incredibly intense. The baby's heart rate dipped low during each contraction, and I was aware of everyone focusing intently on the monitor to see how fast it would rebound. The doctor said the baby was in distress because the amniotic fluid had been contaminated. He was confident, however, that she would be fine, and a short time later, Kim was born. Ten fingers. Ten toes. And she was beautiful.

There was a troublesome looking knot on her head, but the nurses explained that because I did not fully dilate, the contractions had caused her still malleable skull to be pressed against my body. They assured me that it was nothing to be worried about; lots of babies are born with strangely shaped heads, and it would go away after a few days.

Since I had not been able to keep much in the way of food down for nine months, I requested, as soon as the baby was born, to have my first meal. I was ravenous, and I knew that finally, without a doubt, I would actually be digesting this meal.

John carried our newborn daughter to be weighed and measured and showed her off to friends waiting anxiously outside. In the first of many frustrations to come, I nodded off just as the food was brought to me. After I woke up, I cried because the nurse had taken the tray away, then again, I nodded off to sleep.

The nurse woke me sometime later and told me that the baby would not be brought to me for a while. Kim was not yet able to maintain her body temperature, so she had been placed in a neonatal incubator. The nurse repeated that nothing was wrong, and I should not be concerned.

Later that evening, another nurse wheeled the baby and her bed into my room and said, "She's waking up all of the other babies."

I was exhausted and sore from the birth. I had pushed so hard that I had petechial hemorrhages in my eyes, and I felt an incredible burning in my arms. They still shook almost uncontrollably from pulling for leverage, and it was difficult just to lift them for my baby.

The nurse plopped Kim down and trotted out the door. I remember fighting to stay awake in terror that I'd relax, and the baby would roll out of my limp arms to the floor. Fortunately, the wife of John's best friend came to visit. Angela held Kim to let me rest.

When it came time to breast feed Kim for the first time, she seemed uncoordinated and was constantly falling asleep. The nurse was unconcerned when I brought it to her attention. "Oh, that's just postnatal lethargy," she said. She instructed me to thump Kim's feet so she would stay awake long enough to eat.

The next day we brought her home, screeching at the top of her lungs. I figured she was hungry, so I fed her and tried to settle in, but she just didn't calm down. On the third night, I announced to my mom and husband that something was obviously wrong. Kim's behavior was totally different from that of Marcia's, our two-year-old daughter.

Kim frequently startled awake out of sound sleep and began screaming. Because of the long pauses of falling asleep while she nursed, I believed she was tired, although when she awoke during feeding, she appeared to be ravenous. The doctor's diagnosis of colic confirmed my suspicion, so we endured with that understanding.

For the first five days of the week, Kim was awake and screaming round the clock. She then slept for six hours at a stretch for the next 48 hours.

Occasionally, I was fortunate enough to rock her to sleep, to transfer her limp body into her bed, and to quietly tiptoe into my room. I would stretch every muscle to ease into our waterbed without rustling the blankets or rippling the mattress. Feeling confident that she was truly asleep, I'd let myself relax, closing my eyes, feeling my heart rate slow. The sensation, on the brink of sleep, was intoxicating.

Then would come a shuffle and a faint cry. I willed her to go back to sleep, held my breath, waited to hear if she was actually waking up. By then my heart would be pounding, my whole night's rest hanging in balance. "No! No!" I'd silently plead as the pitch in her voice began to rise. "This is torture," I wanted to shriek as I flung back the covers.

The rest of the night I'd pace, bounce, and rock Kim–anything to comfort her. John, unable to sleep, would shout over the screams asking what I thought was wrong and if there was anything he could do. I'd yell back, "I have no idea what's wrong. Try to go to sleep." There was no use in both of us losing sleep.

If I happened to doze off while holding her firmly, and my grip relaxed, she would wake with a jerk, scratching and clutching at my throat as if she were drowning. As she calmed down, she nodded against my clavicle bone, the tiny, bobbing head turning slightly, as she tried to find just the right spot for her nose. After she relaxed, her head as it slowly fell to the side, would startle her awake all over again. Screaming. Always screaming. This was the pattern for many months to come.

Often, when John got up for work in the morning, he found me still rocking the baby, my voice cracking from singing all night long. I'd kiss him before he left. And I'd envy his escape. Shortly after he left, Marcia, who was a lively three-year-old, would be up and fully rested, ready for a day of fun.

Most newborn babies dislike baths, so I ignored Kim's screams of terror as I bathed her, but I did have some cause for alarm when I discovered sores in the pit of her underarms and around the base of her neck. She held her body so stiffly that you could not have inserted a sheet of paper between her arm and body, let alone a baby-wipe or a washcloth. I didn't want to hurt her and was afraid of leaving marks, but the cleaning had to be done.

The sounds in a bathroom bouncing off the slick surfaces and the changes in temperature and texture seemed to terrify Kim. Most babies develop a trusting bond with their mothers. Most babies eventually adjust to these changes in environment and the motions required to go through the bathing process. Most babies remember the bathing experience until it is no longer a terrifying experience. Kim was not most babies; each bath was a horrifying event for her.

When I changed her diapers, I was puzzled by her reaction. There was no appearance of skin irritation, but she reacted as if I were cleaning her with sandpaper instead of a washcloth.

Two weeks after Kim's birth, Marcia was bitten by our basset hound. Marcia's tiny nose sustained an open wound that took eighteen meticulous stitches. The emergency took several hours, and in the end, Angela took care of Kim the rest of the night, so we could focus our attention on Marcia.

John took a week off work to help take care of Marcia's wound, which had to be cleaned several times a day, while I dealt with Kim. Having him home to share the load was wonderful. It cut the burden in half, but the week was over all too soon, and he had to resume his job as a police officer working a new graveyard shift.

I took over the task of Marcia's post-operative care, coping with Kim all the while, and I tried to keep them quiet during the day so John could sleep. It was not long before I was suffering from severe sleep deprivation.

We tried to visit family at picnics during the summer, but the energy it took to attempt to keep Kim quiet was overwhelming. Her screams cut through the vastness of the outdoors. She howled at the wind, the sun, the grass, the world. The family took turns holding her, but there was no comfort for Kim.

We finally came to the point where we declined to go anywhere. We said she was sick, which was what we truly thought; it was obvious that she was in some kind of pain. Perhaps, with time, the problem would work itself out; whatever was wrong would heal or get better. Friends and family came to see her, but no one could speak over the din, and after the first couple of visits, no one stopped by again.

Time blurred for me as days and nights faded into one another. There was no distinguishing in my mind when day time started or when nighttime began. I was always on duty, and I took no notice of whether it was dark or light outside. It was of no consequence to me. As I look back through the first five years of Kim's life, I can only use markers of John's work life to estimate the time of events.

I remember while rocking Kim once, I looked at the bundle in my arms and thought, "Did I have a baby?" I concentrated hard for about two minutes. Then it came to me, "Yes, I did, but who is the other child?" Some time later, I held Marcia in my arms as she slept, and I thought, "This is the one with the injured nose, but who is the other one?" I couldn't even remember their names.

During this blurred period of time, we went to church. I placed Kim in the nursery while Marcia and I attended the service. After the service, Marcia and I went home. About half an hour later, I received a phone call from the nursery attendant.

"Did you forget something?" she asked.

"No, I don't think so." I searched my brain.

"Didn't you forget something at church?"

I *still* didn't tumble on to what she was getting at.

Finally, she said, "Your baby?"

"Kim!" I cried. I had forgotten her completely.

When I got to the church, I was not only embarrassed, but very upset. The church people had quite a chuckle and they assured me that some of them had done the same thing at one time or another, but I was very worried. I took greater pains to keep my thoughts on track and remember that I had a baby!

Crying, crying, never-ending crying. Kim just never stopped crying. John's opinion was to "let her cry it out." We placed Kim in the cradle in and shut the door. It was nerve-racking to sit in the living room trying to pretend she wasn't crying, and I think it is much harder for nursing mothers because of nature's instinct to respond to that sound.

After a while, as if called by the siren's song, I would go lie in front of the bedroom door. I would have no memory of walking to the door. John and Marcia would come and persuade me to rejoin them in the living room, but within a short time, I'd find myself again lying on the cold linoleum floor outside her room.

Soon I started to think of Kim as "The Noise." "The Noise" kept me from getting out. "The Noise" was so awful that my friends stayed away.

After five months of this torture, I couldn't stand it anymore; I needed to stop "The Noise" from controlling my life, to stop interrupting my sleep… just to stop. I went to the cradle and placed my hands on the screaming bundle. In my fuzzy mind, I believed that if I squeezed all of the air out of the lump, "The Noise" would cease. It was not a snap decision. I stood there for quite some time weighing whether or not to stop "The Noise." Some part of me knew I shouldn't, although in my state of mind, I could not reason why. There was an urgency to *do* something, but there was also a feeling that if I did, it would change my life forever.

All of a sudden, like a sleepwalker being awakened from a dream, the fog lifted from my tired, confused mind. I broke into a cold sweat and crumpled to the floor, shaking and sobbing. "The noise" was my *baby*! I fled from the room, horrified at the thought of losing my grasp on reality—horrified at what I'd almost done.

Then and there, I vowed that if that feeling came over me again, I would not go near her, and from then on, whenever I found myself at her door, I turned away to find something—anything to keep my hands busy and my attention diverted.

Even our family doctor could see I was at the end of my rope when I took Marcia in for an appointment. She had caught a cold, and every time she coughed or sneezed, Kim responded as though some internal knife had been twisted. He prescribed cough medicine with codeine to help Marcia sleep, and when I asked if there was anything I could do to help our situation, he advised, "Drink a glass of beer or get a babysitter."

With that advice in mind, John and I decided to hire a babysitter for an evening. Upon the recommendation of a neighbor, we arranged for a teenager to come to our house for a couple of hours. When we arrived home, she greeted us at the door with a blow-by-blow tale of all the screaming. The joy of our two hours away was quickly erased, and after John returned from taking her home, I told him that it was even worse to hear the account than it would have been to endure it.

A more experienced lady sat for us a couple of times later but quit because it was too difficult. We did not try another babysitter for quite some time.

One night John got to the point where he just had to get away. Angela and her husband were gracious enough to invite him over to soak in the hot tub. I urged him to go. There was no sense in both of us staying at home. John had bought some beer so we would have some on hand to take the doctor's advice. As he left, he suggested that I have a beer. The screaming was really getting to me so I decided I would. I drank one and waited a few minutes, but I was no more relaxed than I was before. I drank another one. I had never had much experience with alcohol, so I gulped down yet another.

Unfortunately, I had no concept of time. I had ingested three beers within a matter of minutes. My speech slurred, and the room whirled. When John came home, I met him at the door, tearfully explaining what I had done. I felt ashamed and humiliated. Never again did I try this method of relaxation.

Kim screamed more in public so only in cases of urgency did I take her to the store. The moment we entered the building, all eyes were on us. A friend of mine, a grocery clerk, would use the intercom to call "courtesy" to come help bag the groceries. The box-boys scrambled to get us through the line and our purchases bagged and out to the car. Even when I was alone in the store, I would hear her screaming in my mind. Oftentimes I caught myself tenderly bouncing a ten-pound bag of flour—rocking, swaying, and humming while patting its bottom. If I had a grocery cart, I pushed and pulled it, humming to the contents inside. I'd look around to see if anyone had noticed me, only to find myself doing it again in the next aisle. It unnerved me that I couldn't seem to control my actions.

This lack of control caused me great psychological distress. The lines of reality were blurred, and I'd go from forgetting my baby completely to not realizing that she wasn't with me. Every time I couldn't control myself or my actions, it chiseled away at my self esteem. I was afraid of what I might do—or forget to do—while I was alone and the responsible adult with my children.

While at home, there were times I would let her screech hysterically while I walked slowly around the outside of the house, just to be outdoors and smell the fresh air. It was then that I realized the neighbors could hear her screaming almost as clearly as if she had been outside. What must they think of us? Would they be calling the authorities about suspected abuse? From then on, I was very careful about making sure the children were always clean and properly dressed, paranoid that others would accuse me of child neglect.

A Shift Change

At six months, Kim still appeared to have "postnatal lethargy" while I was feeding her. She fell asleep with her eyes open at least three to five times each time she nursed. She would turn her head away from me, arch her back stiffly, and stare without breaking suction. The strange thing was that it lasted only about a minute and a half. I tried to wait patiently, thumping the soles of her feet to "wake her up," but it didn't work. Then, when she finally became aware of her surroundings, she would cry as though she were hungry. It took forever to nurse her, and it began to injure me.

I went to my gynecologist for treatment during this time, and he asked how things were going. I gave a nervous laugh and told him about the sleep deprivation without elaborating on anything else. I was on the brink of tears. He gave me a stern look and said, "You get some sleep."

"But John's on graveyard... the house...the kids..."

He interrupted me, "I don't care if the house falls down around you. You get some sleep!"

After my treatment was over, I was instructed to take Kim into a secluded room to nurse her. Once again, she "fell asleep." I begged, with tears running down my face while I gently thumped her feet, "Don't, Kim. Please, please don't." (It was later revealed to us that these were some type of seizures that she was experiencing.)

I tried my best to confide in friends and family about what was happening. They had no idea of how things were going at home. How do you tell someone that you came close to taking your own daughter's life? How could you explain that you weren't angry, you were just confused? I tried to test their understanding of our situation by giving some examples of the struggles I had with no sleep or rest. Others felt I was exaggerating the sleep deprivation. They laughed and said that I was just finding out what it was like to be the mother of two children. The comparing of their experience in a typical situation with typical children yielded no grasp or insight of the desperate circumstances in which I found myself. After a while, I kept quiet; no one I knew could relate.

Sometimes the people who are closest to the situation are the last to realize there is a problem. Those who have given birth know that every baby cries and requires a lot of around-the-clock attention. They understand that a new mother is not going to be bright-eyed, well-rested, and springing with energy. Therefore, family and friends are patient and kind because they are aware that this period does not last long, and soon, life will return to normal. But with Kim, life didn't return to what it was before. And it never would.

As time passed, Kim did not slip into any sort of routine. She had her days and nights mixed up. Mostly, she did not sleep at all.

Going without sleep is very difficult until you hit the four-week mark, and the body goes into overdrive. There were certain periods during the day when I would become extremely exhausted. Unable to lie down to rest because of my responsibility, I stayed on my feet. My muscles were sore and stiff. My bones felt dry and grating as if there was no lubricant between the joints. I didn't realize how much sleep a human body requires to regenerate for the next day.

I continually had to fight off the intoxicating feeling of sleepiness. If I were driving during the day, I'd lay my head back on the headrest so I could see beneath my drooping eyelids, but then, after about 10:00 at night, my body would decide that it wasn't going to get any rest, and it pumped adrenaline into my system. I could feel my heart pounding dramatically, and even if I tried to go to sleep, I couldn't. There was no overcoming the racing heart rhythm. Many nights I lay there, trying to will my heart to slow down by concentrating on relaxing thoughts and imagery but to no avail. My body was oftentimes between sleep and a waking state.

After a course of time, the human body realizes it is not going to get a rest period, so it begins to take time out for itself, no matter what its owner is doing. Anytime that I was sitting—in a meeting, a church service, or anyplace where I was not directly and personally engaged—my consciousness would drift. This was different from daydreaming, when a person's thoughts wander away from the subject. It is more like the brain stalls in a groove. I could see where I was, but my mind did not process the information. My brain shut down to its lowest working capacity without going to sleep. Again and again, that feeling of intoxication came over me; I had the sensation of floating while my body felt heavy as lead.

Now, I have never been accused of being the swiftest thinker or sharpest person, but the sleep deprivation caused me to lose a lot of short-term memory and dulled my normally enthusiastic personality. It was difficult to remember a four-digit number or to record withdrawals from the checkbook. Of course, it didn't help that my attention was constantly spliced between the business at hand and what the girls were doing, even without the fatigue.

John was continually frustrated with my lack of focus. There were frequent gaps in our financial records. I was always locking the keys in the car. He thought this would change if I'd just pay attention.

Family and friends became a little less patient and understanding because they thought the baby should be sleeping through the night by now. After all, Kim was over six months old. I knew it sounded like I was complaining about my child, so I stopped reaching out for help in fear of not being heard.

Gradually, the emotional support from family and friends was stripped away. I had no relatives close by who could help. My mother was giving hospice care to her elderly, terminally-ill mother and often asked me to help with her needs. I felt sharp pangs of guilt for turning down her pleas. She, in turn, could not understand why I couldn't put some effort toward Grandma's care. After all, the only thing in my life that had changed recently was that I cared for a baby. I understood how tired my mother was, being short of enough people to supervise around the clock. Making what seemed to her like flimsy excuses put a severe strain on our relationship.

I began to feel hopeless. Things were not going to change. John, not understanding that I was not sleeping while he was at work, was cranky about the condition of the house. Who could blame him? I was embarrassed about it, too. If he came home and did find me asleep, he woke me to inform me that he had worked all day and that I should do my job, too. I felt bad, but under my breath I whimpered, "But the doctor said I should sleep when I could."

Once, when Kim was about ten or eleven months old, I went clothes shopping in an attempt to make myself feel better.

It was hard to believe that the reflection I saw in the mirror was my own. I was not prepared for the hollow expression, the dark circles under my eyes, and the lifeless hair. I knew I hadn't had time to spend on myself, but I wasn't expecting this. Thinking that perhaps it was my attitude, I tried to smile. My face felt like stone, and my muscles were stiff. I couldn't remember the last time I had been light hearted enough to smile. I was past the heartbroken sobbing that revisited me hourly in the beginning. The tears over my circumstances had long been spent and now there was a cold grimness that enveloped me. How could anyone not see the strain on my face?

I sat for a long time in that dressing room saying good-bye to myself. Then I went home, put away my pretty clothes, and started wearing my husband's things.

On a different afternoon a short time later, I had the opportunity to go to K-Mart all alone, just to get out for awhile. I was relieved not to have restrictions on my time, but by the time I had driven three blocks away from home, uneasiness came over me. The farther I drove, the more intense and urgent the feeling became, until I panicked. My heart pounded as though it would burst through my chest. I was gasping for breath and crying without reason. This was insane. The kids were safe at home, and nothing was here to stress me, but all I could think about was turning around quickly and going back. Oddly, I felt that if I could just get home, everything would be all right.

When I arrived, I dashed though the front door. Slowly, the feeling of panic began to recede. John stared at me as though I were crazy. Controlling my voice, I just said that I had changed my mind about the store. I wondered if I'd ever be able to go out by myself again. I was afraid I was mentally ill and was too ashamed to admit it.

John's shift assignments were made on a three month rotation, and shortly after my agoraphobic attack, he was assigned to another three months of graveyard. Once a shift assignment is made, it cannot be changed. John and I now fought constantly. Nearly everything we said to each other seemed to be inflammatory. We argued over who had more sleep or maybe even the most recent shower.

We were both so tired we could barely stand. John confided that on one shift, he had driven through five blocks of traffic lights, and he couldn't remember what color they were or where he was. He also told me that, as he was writing reports, his head hit the steering wheel of his car as he nodded off. I knew as well as he did that this could be lethal, not only for him, but also for the other officers who depended on him for emergency back-up. After hearing this, I made a greater effort to keep Kim quiet so he could sleep. I really believed at the time that all of our problems stemmed from his working that graveyard shift. If only he could change shifts, everything would be all right.

I prayed, pleaded, and begged. I told John again and again to go back and request a change, but each time, he came back with another no, and each time, I fell apart. I knew my limits.

The police department, not understanding our situation, offered us marriage counseling. I just looked at John. We could talk all we wanted. It wasn't going to change Kim.

At one point, John came home for a couple of hours of sleep before he had to go to shooting practice out at the range. Knowing that Marcia would not be up before he had to leave early in the morning and that I would be awake the whole time, he placed the gun on top of our tall bookcase.

I rocked and rocked Kim in the armchair that night. It wasn't working, so I paced with her in my usual routine–bouncing, rocking, and swaying. Suddenly, the gun caught my attention. I examined it from all angles, being careful not to touch it. Deep inside of me, I knew that if I laid my hands on it, I would use it.

All I wanted was to sleep. I had not slept through a whole night more than once in six months. It was so hard to concentrate or think clearly. *If I used the gun,* I thought, *I would have relief from this torture. But if I did, what will have changed? Marcia would not have a mom nor John a wife. I would be dead. But who would take care of Kim? John couldn't take care of her and work, too.*

Satisfied that I had come up with an answer, I sat down again to rock Kim in the recliner, only to find myself again at the bookcase a short time later. My brain had cycled again, and I could not remember the reasons for not using the gun. I spent the rest of the time until John was ready to go out to the range repeating this cycle—having, again and again, to figure out the reasons why I shouldn't touch the gun.

Finally, upon seeing the deterioration of my emotional state (but, even then, not aware of my mental condition), John again approached his boss about changing shifts. The third time John went to his boss, he said he would have to quit if his shift wasn't changed. His boss said again that once an assignment was made, it could not be altered. John tried to explain about the baby. The next question was, "Is the baby sick?" John had to say no, so the problem with the baby just sounded like some lame excuse. A woman police officer stepped forward and insisted that John take her shift. Together, during a long and intense meeting, they persuaded the watch commander to switch shifts.

Battle Fatigue

More than two years later, Kim was finally diagnosed with autism. My sister and her husband opened up their home to me so that I could attend educational seminars. They took care of my children while I learned as much information as possible about the condition that affected my youngest child. My brother in law, Terry, took me out for coffee. When I was fifteen, he had been the youth pastor of my church, and we have a great friendship; I trust him as my confidant. He knows me so well that all he has to do is ask how I am doing, and I pour out my heart. This time was no different. I laid everything out to him: the severe sleep deprivation, the insomnia, the panic attacks, depression, Kim in the cradle, losing my sense of reality and trust in myself, and my fear of losing John and of ruining Marcia. I described everything in detail, so he could understand how it was for me.

While I told him all this, I watched his expression. His mouth was open, eyes staring in disbelief. I couldn't ignore his look of astonishment, so finally, I stopped my monologue and asked, "What? Why are you looking at me that way?"

You know, Eileen," he said as he regained his composure, "As a chaplain in the National Guard, I'm trained to spot signs of stress in soldiers. What you have just described is battle fatigue."

He explained that our bodies aren't made to be on a constant state of alert, and oftentimes, when under extreme duress and fatigue, the body will send out false "fight or flight" responses to ordinary situations. That explained why my heart rate would shoot up for no apparent reason. Why I felt panicky when there was no apparent cause for alarm. Why I couldn't sleep. Why, so many times, when I laid down to rest, my heart wouldn't slow down to a restful enough rate to sleep.

Terry also said that sleep is the way our bodies process the information that we take in during the day. At night, while we are sleeping, our brains sort all of the files and put them in their proper places, so we wake up in the morning, refreshed with our brains rested and ready to receive more information. Whenever I tried to close my eyes to sleep, a series of disjointed thoughts and pictures flickered uncontrollably through my mind like a never-ending slide show. Several times a night, I made myself wake up to clear my mind before trying to go to sleep again, only to have the flickering images return as soon as I closed my eyes. Many times on these nights, I just gave up trying to sleep.

"Battle fatigue," I thought, "How aptly named."

In the past, anyone who got to know me would agree that I was usually a positive, sunshiny, rarely moody person. But now, parts of my inner core–the things that made me Me–were dying, and nothing I could do, by myself, would revive them. I couldn't receive happiness and I couldn't accept or absorb the goodwill of others. While watching a Thanksgiving Day Parade on TV, I just had to shut the set off because the celebration, the joy, the emotion, I couldn't take it in. It was like being a bystander, not being able to participate in a joyful activity. I wanted to feel the lightheartedness of the moment, but was overwhelmed as an incredible stifling blanket of grief that smothered me. My body was reacting to the emotional and mental duress that was ever present. Even though I didn't understand what was happening to me, my body was responding in a very physical way. I began sighing, deep heavy sighing. At first I wasn't aware of my periodic breathing, until I was doing it every three minutes and John calling out from the adjoining room asking me if I was ok. Another issue that plagued me was when I did catch some sleep, I noticed that I woke up with my arms twisted and hands jammed up under my chin in a very stiff and awkward position, my mouth fixed like stone in a grimace. This tenseness in my sleeping position caused my hands and wrists to ache, so I began to wear wrist braces to prevent my hands from curling at night. I didn't have a rational explanation for why my body was acting this way and I had never heard of anyone else having this problem.

I felt a tearing of separation between my former way of being-as a functional adult, and the person who did not possess the power to make changes, who did not have the energy to put her plans into actions, who did not have control over her destiny. Having no real impact on the tiny household around me, I started opting out of making daily decisions leaving any future planning up to my mother and John to decide. Nothing mattered. They could just show me where to stand, and I would be there. My body went through the motions but there was no will of my own. It took too much energy to think, to disagree, to assert myself; as a result, I became passive. I was broken and I didn't know how to fix whatever it was that had altered my mental and physical state. It would take many years, and even then I didn't know if I would ever get the real me back again.

CHAPTER 3

Removing Ourselves
from the Autism Equation

Restructuring Family

If I were to stand back and view the situation, as though I were a consultant giving advice to a client, I would start by telling them to take control of the environment. The reaction to this at first is, "I'm too overwhelmed." "I can't control anything in my life right now. I don't have the energy…I can't." I know this, because I've uttered those very words myself and I am here to say, "YES YOU CAN!" In order to solve any large problem, you have to break it down into smaller parts, then address each issue. It sounds so very simplistic however, when your mind is clouded by lack of sleep, and you don't know where to start, the many pieces of the problem can be overwhelming. The breakdown in personal and family wellness happens when we are unaware that a crisis exists. Parents often try to cope with the new set of difficulties by applying the same problem solving strategies that succeeded in the past with the expectation that their lives will carry on as before; this approach just doesn't work. We have to find a new way of thinking, a new way to restructure our day to day existence.

The treatment for autism should start with the family. I love the quote, "If Mama (or Papa) ain't happy, ain't *nobody* happy." By the same token, we could insert the word "healthy" in that sentence. "If Mama or Papa ain't healthy, ain't nobody healthy." If the life of a parent is in total disarray to the point that it affects their mental and physical health, and cannot function in their daily living routine, then how can they begin to care properly for a child, let alone raise a young one with special needs? Adults need to be able to manage the home environment or it can spiral into chaos and someone will get hurt.

A person who cannot control their body in a space, or does not use tools or equipment as it is intended, can hurt themselves or someone else because they lack self regulation. Until an autistic person learns cause and effect, rules of living in a family or the home structure, they need constant supervision. When I use the term "self regulation," I'm referring to the ability to exert self control or monitor impulsive behavior. This constant supervision can erode the parent's ability to have a constant state of well being.

Parents have the power/authority to build structures, figuratively and literally to keep everyone in the household safe. Before being able to make these changes, they must assess their own challenges, and make time to have the ability to think.

Management

In order for a parent to be healthy, they need sleep, good nutrition, and opportunities for short rest periods during the day, identical to the principles for healthful living that adults advocate when raising children. We as humans cannot survive without sleep. Lack of sleep weakens the body as well as the mind. Adults often rationalize that they will make up the sleep later, they will nibble on something later, they will take that break when they can; and when they are overwhelmed with caring for another, the chance to do so evaporates. With a child who has autism to a certain extent, the parent is *always* on duty. There is no person to swoop in to save you from your situation, so you have to *save yourselves*. Do not feel guilty or selfish. Many parents who have not had a break in such a long time, have cheated their mental and physical states for so long, that they have depleted any reserve energies or resources. They feel a pang of guilt as if they are deserting their loved one, which couldn't be more further from the truth. You have to take care of yourself now so that you can be there for your loved one for future years.

Sleep deprivation

The first and foremost issue that needs to be addressed is sleep deprivation. You can live with a little less food, a little less rest (small breaks during the day), but you *absolutely* require sleep to be able to problem solve, strategize, to make changes to your current environment. The facts of life are, you need oxygen to breathe and you need sleep to live.

Without sleep your short term memory will be stunted to point that you can't remember, thoughts are disjointed and the brain may be unable to retrieve information in a timely manner. Your body will feel heavy and fatigue easily at the smallest of tasks, your joints and muscles will ache. Emotions that you have are intensified, the smallest act of kindness can bring you to tears for hours and something that would have caused you to be slightly angry will make you furious. In my case, going without sleep caused me to have a match light temper. The cruel twist of irony is that a parent can suffer from insomnia despite being so very sleep deprived. Any rest that you are able to obtain, does not offset or mitigate the many hours of sleep that you haven't achieved.

A parent needs to assess why they are sleep deprived. Is it the parent's problem or is it the child? Why is the child having problems with sleep? In our situation, Kim had problems shortly after she was born. In this situation, I would suggest a "sound machine" to mask any ambient noises in the house and neighborhood. Because she had hypersensitive hearing, the noises from blocks away from our house startled her. The remedy would have been to fill the room where she slept with a constant flow of monotone sound, such as white noise or static. Unfortunately, we didn't understand autism at the time and we mistakenly put the fan in *our* room to mask her screaming. Sound machines can be purchased at local stores. They may be referred to as: "Sound Spas," or "Sound Conditioners," and can be found in the infant section, drugstore section or health/wellness areas in your local stores as well as on the internet.

Parents have to protect their ability to sleep and need to set boundaries for others. For example: John's father lived just down the street, and liked to pop in from time to time. This was all very nice and welcome from the time Marcia was born. He did not understand how our circumstances had changed after Kim joined us. Sometimes after a rough night with Kim, I was able to get her to settle down in the late morning hours, which meant I still might salvage some sleep out of the day. His knock at the door sent the household into utter chaos. Kim would start screaming while our dog burst out barking, I was jolted awake just when I was on the verge of sleep. Whenever John was home, not knowing how much sleep I wasn't getting, had no problem waking me to ask a question or to hand me the phone when someone called me on the telephone. He was either away at work or home sleeping while I was dealing with Kim, he took no notice. It wasn't until he found me passed out on the floor, my body could just not keep going any longer, was taking some time out even if I didn't give in to sleep. He took a picture of me lying on the floor because he "thought that was an odd place to take a nap." It took a long time before he finally understood that I desperately needed sleep. He guarded my ability to do so by telling people I was asleep and that they could call back or visit later. With Kim having rotating hours whenever she did sleep, it was unpredictable, when I would get my next break. This frustrated many of our friends and family when they would come to visit and see a note on the door that said, "Do not disturb, SLEEPING!" At first, many people didn't feel the sign applied to *them* after all, certainly it didn't mean them! Finally, we were able to make everyone understand that the rule applied to everybody.

If the issue for the lack of sleep is hyperactivity when the child is older, one of the solutions could be setting up a visual routine or schedule. By having the day broken down into segments which can be visually confirmed continually, gives the autistic person a measure of comfort and stability with routine. Sometimes unexpected disruptions in the routine or highly anticipated events can cause hyperactivity.*

Many uninitiated people may wonder, "What makes the situation different than if it were a typical child staying up at night? Why does a parent need to be attentive when a autistic child is awake?" When a child has a lower development than their chronological age, they can be tall enough to reach things that are harmful. They may have splinter skills meaning, they may not have cognitive abilities for their age, but have very fine motor skills such as unlocking gates, bypassing child safety locks and latches. Some children have a precocious ability in the fine motor skill area, and yet do not have the development to anticipate danger.

Many times in my own situation, when Kim's mind was racing, as she was dashing from one thing to another, she would settle down to watch videos. When I say settle down, it does not mean to sit, but rather she was engaged by the visual images and was more likely not to find activities of her own, like being destructive. She still galloped around the room, jumped off of the furniture, poked my eyes, and drew pictures, always keeping her attention on the tv. I found the longest video possible so that I could catnap on the couch. Never truly relaxing enough into a deep sleep, I continually had my ears tuned for the tale tell sounds Kim crawling over a gate. The absence of noise meant she was occupied with some forbidden object or even worse, her escape.

Parents need to recognize that getting sleep is a high priority. I have given some practical suggestions as to how we handled the situation. There are many more ideas about how to get an autistic child to settle down for sleep. John and I were very passionate about not using chemicals, pills, sleep aides of any kind. We found the greatest success with limiting her stimulation during the day so that she could relax at night. By limiting how many activities for us parents and for her such as playing sports, social dealings, transitions

---

* For more information, refer to "The Girl Who Spoke With Pictures," by Eileen Miller, Jessica Kingsley, Pub. 2008. Pg. 33.

(beginnings and endings of events, running errands), we could control the amount of extra flapping, tip toe walking, circling, jumping or bouncing, her body had to go through before she could settle down for sleep. Simplifying life made her behavior more manageable. It was as though we were tuning into what her body needed. This sounds so childishly easy, but believe me, it is not as effortless as it sounds.

Environment/Safety

In order for a parent to have peace of mind while they are gone to work or even while at home sleeping, their families must have a safe environment. Have you ever tried to do a task when there is a chance that one of your family members could possibly harm themselves or others? It would be very difficult to concentrate. After getting sleep, and the parent's brain better rested, it's easier to take a look around their family's home using a critical eye . Think of the words, "containment" and "safety." Go to a hardware store, electronics department, children's area in a department store or go online to look for various alarms, latches. If the situation is serious, don't be afraid to consider altering the physical structure of the house to make it safe. If you don't own your home, find out what structure the landlord is willing to change to keep your child safe.

For example: I noticed that Kim seemed calmer when she was contained in one room at a time. Early Intervention specialists suggested that having so many rooms available to choose from might be too stimulating. It caused her undue excitement, a type of exhilaration as she wandered and galloped throughout the space. Closing off the rooms by keeping the doors closed cut down on much of the visual stimulation; therefore, it cut down on anxiety and excitement. Kim needed to be able to focus on what was going on in one room only. I attempted to streamline her attention by keeping her enclosed controlled space.

To keep her from escaping, we used safety gates and nursery doorknob covers for years. By the time Kim was between three and a half and four years old, the latest safety latches and structures that we had put into place were being compromised daily. We finally resorted to padlocking the gate across the doorway of her bedroom. After about three days, she came out of her room, took my hand, and smugly placed the padlock into my palm. I was aghast. It was a combination lock; she couldn't possibly have figured out the three-digit number, could she? John changed the combination and within the next three days, she cracked it again. How were we ever going to keep her safe?

We decided to split the girls' bedroom door in half, install the doorknob to lock from the outside, and remove the top half completely, so it wouldn't be a safety hazard. The gentleman at the specialty shop for hardwood doors looked at me as though I was crazy to want to split a perfectly good door. He explained that because my door was hollow inside, it might splinter off and be ruined, but I told him that I had to take that chance. The door, because of its structure, would also have to be plugged where it was cut. I told him I had the utmost confidence in his abilities, left my door with him, went back to my car, and prayed.

We didn't have the money to get a new door. In fact, we really didn't have the money for this. When I came back at the end of the day, the door was ready, plugged and waiting. The man told me that the glue wasn't quite dry, but as long as no one was swinging on it, it would be all right. I was so happy that I gave this stranger a hug before I toted the halves of my door to the car. By the time I got home, John was installing the extra needed hinges.

We placed Kim into her room with her new door. She was unhappy because she couldn't see through it as she could the gate. I stayed at the door and talked to her so she would know she hadn't been abandoned, but she acted miserable until I distracted her with a cookie. Then she went on playing in her room.

Having her securely penned in lasted for about a week before she began to lift her leg above her head onto the doorknob and scale with her other leg over the door. During another respite planning session, we found a different solution. John picked up a motion detector alarm from the local electronic store. I attached Velcro to the door and to the back of the alarm. We placed the alarm just below the doorknob on the outside. Then, anytime she rattled the doorknob, bumped the door, or tried to climb it, the alarm gave a piercing shriek. It taught her cause and effect as well as giving me a cue to go check on her whereabouts.

Plan a Time to Think

Not every house plan is like the layout of our home, so each place is very individual, what may work for one family, may not apply to another. In this instance, I would draw out the floor plan of the house and give some thought to "containment. Then I would walk around inside and outside the building seeking to pin point problematic areas. I would advise to plan out what you can do as a temporary fix and what you would contemplate doing in a permanent situation. This does not mean that the child will only be kept in one room for the rest of his or her life, just in one room at a time. By putting up gates, locks, door alarms, a parent is corralling the child into one room so that the focus for the child is not on escaping from the area, but on being in that safe space and feeling secure.

When it comes to electronics in a child's room such as a TV, DVD player or stereo, I would have an electrician move the outlet up high on the wall and place the electronics on a shelf or better yet, mount it to the actual wall. This way there are no wires for the child to get into and no outlets in which to stick objects. You may feel this is quite drastic, but then again, you have to consider whether this is a temporary issue or a more permanent one. The expense of such a measure may be well worth your while in the peace mind and protection or cost of your electronics.

Furnishing the House

We took into account Kim's penchant for staying up late at night when we purchased a couch. As a baby, up to the time she grew too heavy for me to breathe, she slept on my chest, and as she grew taller, we could no longer fit on the same couch. The older she became, the less sleep she required, and she spent most of the night bouncing and galloping around the room. However, if she did finally settle down, there just wasn't room on the old couch. I tried John's reclining rocker for a time, but nothing really helped her sleep. She leapt from one piece of furniture to another which, had she not been so adept, it could have ended in disaster. We began to limit how many pieces in the room. I noticed that the more sparse the room, the calmer she became.

The answer to our problems was a sectional couch. We could arrange the long couch so that it would fit both of us without Kim disturbing my sleep. While we were shopping for this couch, the clerks at furniture stores grew extremely frustrated because we had certain specifications: The couch couldn't be too stimulating to look at; certain patterns disturbed Kim. It had to be soft; a rough weave irritated her hypersensitive skin. It couldn't be loosely woven; she would pick at it. And finally, it had to be durable; the way she galloped and perched was rough on the springs and material.

We finally settled on a large, light-blue sectional with foam cushions; soft, rounded edges; and no exposed wood, in case she fell against it. All of us could fit on the couch at the same time with plenty of room for anyone to stretch out and take a cat nap. The couch eliminated the need for a number of pieces of furniture, so we put away our thoughts of any particular style or motif for the room. Anything of merely sentimental or real financial value had already been put away years ago, and we had also clipped all of the cords of the mini-blinds so that they would not pose a hazard for hanging or choking.

We had childproof locks and latches on each and every cupboard door and drawer even though Kim did not have free access of the house. And yes, there were times in the course of my day as a housewife that I would break down and cry from being a little "latch happy" from locking and unlocking all day long. The important thing was that we made the necessary changes to make the safest environment possible for everyone's well being.

(**Attention!** as a side note: Whatever structures that are built into the house, Fire safety is a must! ***Before placing locks or latches consider what will be done in case of fire.*** If you do have locks on your doors, check with your local fire department to see if they have a computerized log of residences. Some fire departments have this capability. You may be able to get them to make a notation so that safety officials are aware that locks, latches and gates that are used on doors *inside* the house. *There are stickers available on the internet to inform fire department of a special needs person in residence. (All families should practice fire scenarios/plans for their house, especially those with special needs.)

Mother's Helpers

As we grow up throughout our lives, we find that in order to go about our day or to accomplish many tasks during the period in which we are awake, we need to set aside time or at least commit to focus on one task at a time in such a way that we can compartmentalize the segments in our day. When we get older in adulthood, we are more efficient, learning to multitask do two or more jobs simultaneously. We switch from one environment to the next, doing the jobs we need to at home and then onto work or running errands. As adults we take care of the kids, clean house, go to work or stay at home to work, get meals, clean ourselves, and function to get what we need in our every day responsibilities. Accomplishing these tasks is all contingent on being able to finish the job without interruption, being able to have peace of mind that family is safe, and the focus to do so. My attention was constantly spliced between trying to make dinner and constantly leaving my project to get the child down from climbing the bookcase or sweeping a child's mouth to ensure that there is nothing to choke on or be poisoned with. Now most people will tell you that it is perfectly normal, that all children interrupt or take time and focus away. Ok. I will give you some examples:

I often had to wait for someone to drop by my house or even phone a neighbor to come look after my child while I went to use the bathroom. I couldn't take Kim in with me because she was frightened of the space; she flung herself on the floor in a tantrum because I touched her and with her flailing around in such a small enclosed space, she was slamming her head between the bathtub and the sink cabinet.

One day, when she was 3 ½ years old, Kim indicated that she wanted to go outside to play in the sandbox. I had many things to do that day, and it seemed that my life had boiled down to just one thing: watching that kid! Knowing that she stripped off her clothes because of tactile sensitivity, the autism specialist suggested that we dress her in a worn-out, oversized T-shirt. I dug around through some of John's shirts that had seen better days. One of these was particularly soft. It had some small holes, but I figured no one was going to see her in the backyard, anyway. There were two locks on the small garage door and two locks on the side gate leading to the front yard, and I made sure they were all secure before I let her out to play, and then I stood at the window watching her for about five minutes.

John's uniform needed to be pressed, so I brought out the ironing equipment, but I checked on Kim about every three minutes. Each time, I'd find her out there happily chattering to herself. This was ridiculous, I thought. I wouldn't get anything done at this rate. I decided to check at five minute intervals instead of three.

I checked after the first five minutes. So far, so good. Then she made her move. During the second five-minute interval, she disappeared. I ran out and examined the yard and then the entrances. The gate was wide open. I yelled for Marcia, and she, knowing the drill, began to assign the neighbors, both young and old, specific areas to search.

I stayed close, clutching the phone in case someone found Kim. After she'd been gone an awfully long time, and no one had located her, I started to venture down toward a row of houses by the river. Ironically, most of the houses closest to the river had swimming pools, and Kim was so attracted to water that it only made sense to search there first. I went around beating on doors, trying to raise someone—anyone—and getting no answer. Even if nobody was home, I thought, Kim could be in the back of one of these houses, already drowned in one of the pools.

I finally found a house where someone was home, and I know I sounded like a crazy woman, talking as fast as I could, still grasping my phone. Two men were there, and one of them ran over to the house next door to check the pool while the other jogged around behind his house and down the path to the river. Neither found her.

I asked if I could use their phone because mine was too far from the base to be any good, and I phoned 911. Before dispatch could really ask me any questions, I blurted out information: "This is John's wife. He is on duty now.

His daughter is missing. She is three years old, blonde, blue-eyed, about 34 pounds. She has a mole…"

I was almost finished with my frenzied description before I heard the voice on the other end of the line saying, "Eileen, we've got her! Do you hear me? Listen! WE'VE GOT HER! John is on his way." The dispatcher gave me the address where Kim was.

As I hung up, I was embarrassed that these total strangers had to witness this little drama, but they wished me well as I set out to locate Kim. Unfortunately, I was so rattled that I couldn't remember the exact address, and I just wandered around trying to find the right house. Finally, I asked another stranger if I could use his phone and called dispatch back. They instructed me to go home, and John would bring Kim to me there.

I jogged back to the house and told the neighbors on our street that Kim had been located. Then I complimented Marcia on her level-headedness. She had done her job well.

Kim was actually smiling as she rode home in John's police car. After we all met in the living room, John told me the neighbors' perception of this ragged waif. They had been gardening in their front yard when a little child began to play with their dog. The child spotted a small wading pool and began to strip off her T-shirt. Apparently torn between dashing to the large swimming pool in the backyard or wading in this smaller pool, she wisely chose the little one. She splashed and danced in the water while this family began to gather around the tiny visitor, wondering who she was and where she came from. As they looked at her and at one another, Kim chattered and cooed.

"I think she speaks Chinese!" the little boy said.

"It's not Chinese, but it is nothing I've ever heard before," remarked the mother.

Kim hopped out of the pool, walked through the back of their house, opened the refrigerator, and helped herself to the milk before they spotted the identification bracelet on her wrist and called 911 to report a found child. Dispatch said they'd send an officer to take the report.

As soon as I called, they knew whose child it was and sent John. When John arrived, the people of the house said that they felt they should report child neglect. "Just look at her ratty clothes—and no one has even come to look for her." Evidently, as I was knocking on their front door, they were around back trying to catch up to Kim and couldn't hear my frantic pounding.

John was too embarrassed to admit that this was his own child. He said he would look into it and left with Kim.

My ability to accomplish everyday mundane tasks that everyone takes for granted was hugely compromised. I needed help in order to compartmentalize my life so I could function.

One of the ways that I learned to cope with the extra load of responsibility of being ever watchful of Kim, was to invite a 12 or 13 year old girl to help me out with some of my duties as a mother. It is an ideal time for girls because they are not yet distracted by boys and growing up. Young teenage girls still have enough childhood in them to be interested in having fun and helpful, yet possess the energy to match a hyperactive toddler. They are quite observant, an excellent quality to have, and they take the rules seriously. One of my steadfast rules of the house was, absolutely no purses in the house. Someone had recommended that we have an adult friend of theirs become a Respite Care provider. We decided to try her out. She brought in her purse to which I requested that it stay out in her car. She said that she had seizure medication in it and had to have it with her at all times. Against my better judgment and a little voice screaming inside me, I allowed her to put it on top of the bookcase which was 4 feet high, far out of Kim's reach. When we came home, Kim had something white in her mouth. I inquired as to what it was, ever aware of what was going into it. The care provider brushed it off as "a piece of candy." I asked if she gave her candy, because we didn't have any candy and as we wrestled it out of Kim's mouth we found a tiny pill, seizure medication. It was not the first and only time that adults just would not listen to the stringent rules that were made to protect Kim from herself. It was after this that Kim's EI teacher suggested her 12 yr. old daughter come to work for us.

Looking after Kim was physically draining, but from the time Kim was diagnosed until she was about four-and-a-half years old, Hannah, volunteered as a mother's helper to help keep track of Kim, to help her transition in public, and to hold her so that my hands and attention could be free to focus on Marcia. Whenever assistance was needed, such as in the family function of giving Kim a bath, dosing her with medication, or coaxing her into the car, Hannah was there. She had a genuine interest in children. We opened up our hearts and home to her; there were so few people we could let into our circle at that time.

Hannah accompanied us on a couple of trips to the coast and once on a two-day trip over the mountains. We hadn't felt such freedom in years. Staying overnight in John's relatives' house was draining because Kim couldn't sleep; the different environment caused her to be hyperactive. Hannah would stay up with her part of the night, and then I would take over. The watch was necessary not only to keep Kim safe and out of their belongings, but also to keep her quiet so everyone else could sleep. Unfortunately, there was no

VCR, no cable TV, and no computer to help Kim to focus. Their home was very still–no noise to mask the sounds of her movement–so keeping Kim silent and entertained was doubly difficult. By morning we were both very tired.

No napping was possible during the day as relatives wanted us to see the town, picnic, and engage in lively conversation. Hannah and I took turns resting throughout the day, spent another night maintaining Kim, and, finally, welcomed the daybreak. After breakfast, we piled into the van, where Hannah and I alternated between paying attention to the girls and drifting to sleep.

Rest areas were difficult because, once she was in the van, Kim didn't want to get out, and after being out of the car, she didn't want to get back in. Hannah was instrumental in defusing frustrating situations and was able to wheedle Kim into the car so we could get on our way. There was only one other person besides our relatives with whom Kim would have such a trusting relationship: a neighbor girl who, like Hannah, had an interest in our girls. We met Mariah before the girls were born, when she was quite young.

As we became consumed with raising our family, we were nearly unaware of how time had passed. Suddenly, it seemed, Hannah was ready to move on to teenage interests. Although we lamented the fact that Hannah would not be so often available to assist us, we certainly understood.

While I was talking to a neighbor about our dilemma, she reminded me that Mariah had grown up quite a bit and might be interested in helping us out. We were so fortunate! Mariah's mother worked in a group home with the disabled and had experience with and extensive knowledge of autism.

Again, someone had come to our aid to help Kim go to public places and attend respite camp and to give us some intensely needed breaks. One year when Kim was 4 years old, Mariah volunteered to work a Respite Care day. It was Christmas time and our local respite care providers planned a whole six hour period where children with all kinds of disabilities were invited for a day of fun, games and crafts. The parents had some time off from the intensive care and responsibilities of their children. I for once was at ease after all, Mariah had been with us for quite some time. When I went to pick up Kim, she seemed happy. After a block or two of driving down the road, I noticed her head started to nod. Kim never fell asleep in the car. Immediately upon arriving home, I called the Respite Care Coordinator whose name was Tami. I told her that I needed to know if Kim poisoned herself and then filled her in on the details. Tami assured me that it was impossible; she had assigned Mariah to shadow Kim the whole time. There must have been some mistake, it just wasn't like my child to drift off to sleep. Tami laughed and again assured me that everything was ok. She had watched Mariah as she followed my little girl throughout the whole time. "I can tell you why Kim is so sleepy. She tried every doorknob in the two story church for over 6 hours." "And Kim didn't walk from door to door….she galloped."

I longed to do the things that I would have ordinarily done with my girls had circumstance been different. Rolling out dough and baking cookies was such a simple thing to do, but it took more than one person to make certain that it was a safe activity. There was the heavy rolling pin, an object that could be weaponized which needed to be managed. A watchful eye to make sure Kim didn't wander into the kitchen where the oven was hot. The hand over hand activity of stamping out the cookies with metal cutter had to be handled carefully, which if frustration flared, could become airborne.

The mother's helpers were never left alone solely in charge of my girls, but to be an extra pair of eyes, ears, and hands. After several months of training these girls, they were ready to take on the responsibility for a few hours. It is ironic how with an adult, I would leave 2 pages of instructions which was barely glanced over, whereas these young women had committed the rules to their hearts.

We came to know Mariah and Hannah as trusted friends. As time went on, we able to train a number of women who we literally entrusted our girls lives. Although we had fun, these girls performed serious and often exhausting work. They received on the job experience that was challenging and letters of recommendation whenever needed Without these extraordinary young women, we would not have been able to accomplish the everyday things that most families take for granted: a family walk in the park, a shower, a sane moment to have quiet thoughts without being consumed by the safety concerns and needs of another. They were an integral part of bring our family balance back to the center where it belonged.

Depression and Grief

When I refer to the onset of my circumstance with depression, it is not a preexisting condition but rather is brought on after having a child with special needs. In my case, severe sleep deprivation, isolation, and lack of compartmentalization of my situation caused me to have a decent dose of depression. My world had drastically changed from being a young mother who would grow into the role of responsibilities, to a mother who had intense responsibilities thrust upon her. Add on top of all of that, dealing with a child who I did not understand, unaware of the hidden disability, trying to keep everyone safe, learning a different way of parenting and communicating. I was cut off socially, not by any intentional cruel act, almost like I was selected out of my social culture. I felt I no longer belonged.

I was in a survival mode. I couldn't see past the walls of my home. It came on so gradually, that I couldn't identify it within myself. Thinking that my panic attacks, my dream like state between awake and asleep was mental illness, I tried to hide it from my husband and family.

I had not shared anything of what went on in our home with anyone but my brother in law. It wasn't until I was invited to go to a grieving workshop for parents of children with disabilities. The reason I decided to attend was to learn about grief so that I could understand and maybe lend support to those parents whose children had a more serious condition than my daughter. The presenter announced that she was a grief counselor from the local hospital and usually talked to people after they suffered the loss of a loved one. In large letters on an easel directly in front of me, I could see terms like sleep deprivation, hallucination, memory loss, insomnia, and depression. As she went over the material, she summed up my life for the last four years. She went into great detail about those symptoms being part of a normal and natural grieving process.

She also pointed out that the closer in time a parent is to a critical event such as a hospital stay for physically fragile children—or in the case of autism, an escape or a violent episode—the more intensely he or she will experience depression. As the time between crises becomes less, the cycles of depression become more and more intense.

The woman talked about how holidays and birthdays bring on cycles of depression and grief. They are anniversaries of the loss of a loved one, or in our case, reminders of how our children had not progressed. In my own mind I was reflecting on gifts of clothing hung in the closet never worn and toys that were never touched. The feeling I had, even months and years later, when seeing these gifts tore at my heart. Every parent enjoys giving gifts to their children, and they usually come pretty close to guessing what would bring the light of joy to the child's eyes. Not so with Kim. I approached shopping for her with apprehension. There was no way of knowing what she would like, and she hated surprises. Toys were either absorbed by Marcia's collection or given away.

The toys we bought scared Kim. At the age of two, she shrieked in horror as we opened a door revealing a toy wheelbarrow for Marcia and a bubble lawnmower that made clicking sounds for Kim. She would retreat into the house and hide behind John's chair as Marcia exclaimed in joy and ran to play with her new toy. For a while, Kim would even avoid going outside because she knew the new toy was out there.

At first, we didn't allow Marcia to play with Kim's toys, hoping that Kim would get used to the idea and learn to enjoy the toys, but as time went on, we gave our assent. Sometimes, by the time Marcia was allowed to play with them, even she would already have lost interest, so some toys were never touched.

Those untouched toys sitting out in the yard or the corner of the porch haunted me, too. They were a source of pain. It wasn't just the sting we felt when our gifts were rejected. It wasn't even the pang of disappointment at spending the precious bit of money we had managed to save. The pain cut deeply into us as each gift-giving time marked the passage of time and underlined the progress that Kim was not making.

If Kim had been the typical child we had expected, she would have enjoyed these things. It was as if a child born full of promise had ceased to exist. I had lost something, but I couldn't quite understand just what it was that I had lost or when and how I had lost it. It was not really like experiencing a death, but the gnawing emptiness that deepened as time went on was surely a profound sense of loss. All I could understand was that the clothes hanging undisturbed in the closet haunted me and made me feel like the child the clothes were intended for was gone.

I was completely enthralled as the grief counselor opened my life like a book and started to interpret and connect my emotions with reasoning. All that I had been through was rational, it all made perfect sense, not excuses, but sense! I felt that she was speaking directly to me, and relief washed over me as I sat there; I *wasn't* mentally ill.

After physically making changes to our home environment, getting the sleep and the help I needed, I still had one more challenge to deal with. In my case, severe sleep deprivation, isolation, and lack of compartmentalization of my situation caused me to have a deep depression. I had never experienced any type of depression before, after all, I was eternally optimistic. After Kim was born, and all of the stress with her newborn autism issues as well as the trauma that Marcia experienced 2 weeks later, I was taken over by a horrible depression that would not lift. Although I was experiencing symptoms of depression, I couldn't identify it in myself. I cried countlesss times a day even though I couldn't attribute it to any cause. As I bustled around the kitchen doing chores, I sighed constantly in strange intervals, for no reason. My lungs felt heavy and my shoulders slumped as though carrying a heavy burden.

After I was able to identify my struggle with depression, I began to come to grips with my situation. I was not as frightened, now that I knew it was all natural and normal. Now that I understood where the feelings were coming from, I could cope with them accordingly.

First of all we started with a healthy, functioning, loving, intact family whose struggles in life at this point, were basically financial, with average fluctuations in daily stress. The whole family was well rested, fed and had the emotional support of extended family and friends.

If any parent who is in control of creating an environment for the family is struggling with their mental and emotional wellness, then how can children learn healthy coping or problem solving skills? Let's face it; we all have rough patches when we are going through challenging circumstances at various times in our lives. When we as parents feel our back is against the wall and we have no more resources left, there are "strategies for change, because the alternative is unacceptable." That is when we tap into our reserves and find our steely strength.

I've heard it time and again as people puzzle over why a child with autism can be so challenging for a parent to deal with. After all, there are kids with all kinds of disabilities that require extra attention, training and parenting skills. After reading of a tragedy involving a parent and an autistic child in the news media, a person has to wonder, "How does a situation get into this state? What makes the needs of an autistic child any different than a child of another disability? These are the questions I would have been asking myself before I became a parent of an autistic child, before my reserve tank hit empty.

When a father or mother or both are having problems coping with day to day life, the primary structure of the family starts to deteriorate. It is up to the adults to provide a physically and emotionally safe environment for their children. Parents need to learn how to provide the same type of household for themselves.

There are many ideas about how to structure the family environment for the needs of an autistic child. When first considering strategies or systems for change, there are some questions that should be considered.

- Will the proposed system fit into my family's lifestyle?
- Am I willing to continually support this strategy?
- Will it be adaptable to other environments or for future use?

Since I did not have the first clue about how to choose a strategy, there were so many.

Positive reinforcement is so very important. Rewards must be given immediately in order for the connection between the desired goal being completed and the reinforcement. It was difficult trying to think of what would motivate my toddler to try to do anything. The things that enticed Kim into action could be counted on one hand. I read many books with different ideas about ways to get autistic children motivated to achieve goals. One of the strategies was to toss the child up in the air lightly. I decided that would be one that could work for Kim. The teacher told me to consider this carefully. How many times a day or per hour was I willing or physically able to do this? My daughter was only 3 yrs. old at the time, she was light. The preschool teacher pressed the point. How long until Kim would be too big to be able to do this? It was not a practical strategy. We settled on a simple container of bubble liquid. They were a portable bottle of motivation. The bubbles were round, iridescent, floating and exciting as far as most children are concerned. It was the perfect solution for a few years until we found other age appropriate motivators.

Some of systems or strategies involved setting up symbols all over the house to help cue children into what tasks they should be doing. I seriously considered this until her teacher sat me down to think about what this actually meant. She asked me if I was willing to set up my whole house with these paper symbols. I replied yes. Then she asked, "How would Kim be able to navigate the environment in someone else's house if she went for a visit?" My daughter would be dependent on the symbols, and actually limited her to only environments set up for her. No matter how much I was willing, I couldn't make the system work for every situation. The teacher pointed out that I "couldn't change the world for Kim." She told me that the way to look at it was to consider ideas of how we could get my daughter to adapt to the world around her. I learned how sort through the numerous established systems developed to add structure to home life that would work best for my lifestyle.

Recap:
Identify the Problem
Control the Chaos
Make Changes in Environment (permanent or temporary)
Reestablish Compartments in your life by using Mother's Helpers
Recognize Signs of Depression and Grief
Can't Change the World, Fit Your Lifestyle

NOTE: Anyone experiencing symptoms of severe sleep deprivation or depression should seek help from a medical or mental health professional.

CHAPTER **4**

Journal Examples

Now that we have made changes in order to get some meaningful sleep, we can consider strategies regarding alteration of our household to keep the children safe. By improving our mental health and physical wellness, we can concisely concentrate our efforts on autism.

Think of family stresses and strains, ups and downs, ebb and flows, as being a background noise or commotion that is distracting to a person who has hypersensitive hearing. Inconsistency and unpredictability in routine daily life causes excitement, anxiety and confusion, which makes it difficult for an autistic person to attend to important information amidst all of the diversions. Tactile stimulation such as clothing, the nearness of someone's arm brushing the skin ect… can fracture an autistic person's focus. Barking dogs, ambient noises like fans, heaters, fluorescent lighting can cause an incredible distraction and disruption to the learning process. Sensory issues are popular areas to examine when addressing stimulation, but by the same token, we should also scrutinize the effect of the changes in scheduling (routine) and introductions of persons in the immediate family circle. For example, the introduction of a new relationship into the family unit such as dating or has short term friendships, can add an element of stimulation. A new individual occupying/sharing the familial space can change the orientation or dynamics of the room for a person with autism. The sudden introduction of the stimulation can have a positive or negative effect which doesn't matter, the fact remains that change is ever present. If these alterations in daily life were charted on a graph, so that a person could see the stimulation, it would show erratic spikes correlating with the changes of the day, much like a seismograph that charts earthquake events. Unlike the experts in the field of earthquakes, we could predict a precursor or reaction to a change in routine. By understanding what caused the reaction to changes, we could prepare Kim for variations in her life and thereby cut down needless stimulation and unpredictability.

By removing the element of irregularity in an autistic individual's life, they can better centralize their attention *on learning* rather than the continual disturbance of family life, which can create a barrier *to learning*. This creates a more concise, laser sharp focus on the tasks and goals that lay before them.

One of the best ways I can illustrate the concept of removing unimportant information from daily life is to relate this story:

This past year my sister bought a property in Oregon. She had been in the large city of Washington DC. for many years and was ready for some rural life. Next to the house that she bought, was a beautiful orchard. It was springtime in Oregon and as a result of the annual rainfall, the plant life was thriving. She exclaimed to me how lovely it looked as she glanced over the orchard with the trees, the buds breaking open, there was a thick carpet of daisies and clover beneath. The next day, she heard the noise of a tractor. Much to her dismay, she found that the farmer had mowed all of the beautiful flowers below the trees. She couldn't understand why anyone would want to cut down the flowers, they weren't that tall and they weren't invasive. She phoned me up the next day to tell me what she found out after striking up a conversation with the farmer when he was finished putting his tractor away for the day. Apparently there was a good reason for getting rid of the carpet of flowers.

He said that he kept many hives of bees for the purpose of pollinating his orchard. He pointed to the boxes where he kept them at the other end of the orchard. When the daisies and clover are blooming under the trees, the bees can become distracted from their intended target, and work on the flowers instead. Every year he mows everything below the trees so that the bees go straight to their work. He wanted them to seek out only the trees…. only the trees…only the trees. This stuck in my mind as my sister was sharing her story. It struck a chord within me. This is what I had been doing with Kim all of these years. I sorted what information we gained from her and for her. I had to consider what important information she was giving us amongst the myriad of responses we received from her in various different environments and stimuli. Secondly, to figure out what could I do to mow down the unimportant information that distracted her so she could focus on the target, *learning!*

Much of our autism journey points back to the very roots of learning which was in the Early Intervention Infant/Toddler program. Even though they did not have the all the answers regarding how to go about dealing with a child who had autism, they showed me the proper tools to get there. At the suggestion put forth by an Early Intervention Specialist, the indispensible tool of the daily journal was borne.

I was a bit bewildered as to why I needed to purchase a spiral notebook for Kim's preschool class. Perhaps the teacher would be taking notes about lesson plans. When I inquired, the teacher told me to write *my* observations. "Of what?" I thought. It seemed rather vague, but as always, I was ready to comply with anything to move Kim forward. She was 3 years old and had basically no communication system except for throwing a tantrum when she was frustrated. She had learned through the summer, after graduating from the infant/toddler class, to initiate sounds, but she still could not be understood. I began….

Getting to know Kim
This was the first journal entry of what would be years of communication between the teachers and me:

Sept. 3
These are phrases that Kim uses:
"gold-gold-gold fish"
"a down stairs"
"Christmas play"
Eileen

I thought that if the teachers were familiar with some of her words, they could work them into conversation and encourage her to talk.

Journal topics covered such things as toilet habits, events of the day, language and information on interaction, strategies for communication, and schedules. When Kim came home from school, she was unable to tell me about her day, by way of the journal entries, the teacher filled me in on Kim's days at school. She observed Kim's likes and dislikes and her emerging skills. This is how John and I began to get to really know our child—when she was four years old. We narrowed our focus to who she was and who she was not. It didn't matter about the description of autism or where she fit on the spectrum, we wanted to know the person who was inside.

My favorite part of the day was when Kim came home with her backpack. I would dig through her changes of clothes, diapers, and lunch items in search of the notebook. Each day's entry page was paper-clipped so we could turn to it immediately. Simple notes told us of Kim's accomplishments and classmates she had brief interactions with, as well as suggesting possible words or phrases to use to reinforce or ask about her day. Although if other people had read the entries, they would have found them very mundane, it was all music to my heart.

We wrote down games that we played with Kim. As a way of communicating with her, John encouraged her to sit on his lap, and she initiated one game by opening her hand. He copied the motion. I logged one of their games down in the journal:

> She says "open." Quickly, she closes her hand. She says "close." He copies it. They repeat this many times until she tires of it. Perhaps the teachers could ask her some questions about it to spark a response.

Her words were not always clearly enunciated when she spoke. Sometimes she sounded like she had a mouthful of rocks, and depending on how much stimulation she had been exposed to that day, she might be jutting her chin and grimacing, which made clear speech even more difficult, but still, she was speaking in this game, and we could understand what she was saying.

It was through the writings we discovered that Kim was more distracted by daytime stimulation and could concentrate much better between the hours of 2:00 and 5:00 a.m. when most of the neighborhood was asleep. I found, during these late hours, that when I stood beside the TV and signed to her some of the scenes from the movies she frequently watched, she learned the hand gestures more quickly.

There were so many things about Kim we didn't know. It wasn't from the lack of interest; we just didn't know how to unlock the information. At one point, Mary wrote in the notebook that Kim's favorite color was green— electric-lime or neon green. By that time, we had learned so much from the teachers about how to motivate Kim to do what we wanted her to do, that we had even begun to get creative, so with that favorite color tidbit tucked away in our arsenal, we concentrated on finding objects of that color.

We learned that a corn chip was her favorite snack food, that the color of red meant "hot," and that her favorite book at the time was *Mouse Train Ride*. We also discovered that she preferred to be called Kim rather than "Kimmie," as we had always called her. Even though her "baby book" was not filled with notations like: baby's first smile, first giggle, first word, first kiss, the journal contained beautiful stories of the moment when she discovered, "night-time"(discovery of it being dark outside) and of when she understood the sign language word for "sky." In essence, the journal helped assuage the feelings of missing out on the milestones that parents celebrate with their typical children. It was an unexpected benefit of logging in notes on the daily life of my daughter. I felt warm that I recaptured what I had lost, at least part of the person who was known as Kim was contained between the pages of paper.

Mary began sending mystery items home from school in her backpack to reinforce this naming. Usually, the item was just an ordinary object she was familiar with, and I'd ask her what it was or what she did with it, in order to stimulate conversation. The important lesson learned in this exercise was that an entry in the journal from the teacher clueing the parent in on the name of the object and what particular words were used in describing these mystery objects. Sometimes I didn't know what they were myself!

One of the most important aspects of the journal was to record bits of language, because Kim verbalized infrequently, we needed to know if there was a reason for her to speak and if we could know that, perhaps we could recreate the environment to have it occur more frequently. She also did not enunciate clearly. Coordinating the many muscles of the mouth and tongue to form a word is a pretty awesome feat when you think about it. Any spontaneous speech was a laborious task for her. The listener had to be very patient. However, she did speak in a tongue that has yet to be identified. When she was in preschool, she uttered a phrase over and over in a sing-song kind of way, "Nee nee nee na pount, a pount." She repeated it for hours until I thought my brain would bleed. I logged the phrase into the notebook, but unfortunately no one could ever pinpoint what it meant. Only Kim would know and she wasn't able to share her secret joy of that phrase. There was another expression that she seemed to be enamored with that was also written down in hopes of discovering the meaning. This one has a rhythm or beat to the sentence; "Da cane, da cane, sa fossa, fossa bags." Again it was uttered over and over, not in any certain area of the house, not during the watching of videos, not to any certain person. She had an obsession with several video tapes, and out of our vast collection, it would be difficult to nail it down. She said it again, "Da cane, da cane, sa fossa, fossa bags." Something clicked in my brain. It must be a line that I heard from somewhere. I quickly pulled out the video tapes, scattering them carelessly as I was frantically searching for the right one. There were so many. I found it and popped it into the machine and fast forwarded to the part. I pushed play and the Grinch character in the movie "The Grinch Who Stole Christmas," says the line, "It *came* without ribbons, it *came* without tags, it *came* without packages, boxes or bags." I found it! It all made sense, even though it wasn't Christmas time. She did have an obsession about that particular movie and many of her drawings depicted scenes from that story. Kim seemed quite pleased that I now understood. I wrote down bits of language trying to decode the meanings. It was vital that any connection, any way we could convey to her that we shared communication, the closer we were to penetrate Kim's inner circle. The fact that she had been drawing many pages devoted to that movie theme was only portion of the puzzle just like the journal had provided only one part as well. I needed all of the tools at my disposal to piece together this very complex child.

Interestingly enough, getting to know my daughter more personally wasn't the only benefit of writing in the journal. We found patterns of behavior that altered drastically during the changing of the seasons. This was such a valuable discovery because we could pinpoint and anticipate when she would be less flexible in her routine and her temperament. She became more obsessive and her autistic behavior became more intense during this time. She regressed in speech and language, toileting, sleep patterns were disturbed and her ability to handle transitions or alterations in scheduling was sorely absent. One fascinating fact was that her drawings became more three dimensional and detailed. As a result of this change in her schedule/orientation of the world, expectations had to be lowered only for a short time. We also discovered that after she had a regression, she had an incredible learning spurt. We could then take advantage of this window in time where she seemed to take in information more readily. This would never have been discovered had it not been for the journal. I must express to you how instrumental the observations, noted daily (sometimes hourly), added to our knowledge of Kim, her learning patterns, the ebb and flow of her autism. As time went on, the significance of the journal came to light.

A Hurt of the Heart

One of my most favorite of all the stories about journal writing is one particular incident which really highlights and exemplifies the importance of having a journal go between home and school.

It was just after the winter break in Kim's kindergarten year. At first though there were some rough patches with Kim adjusting to new schedule, new people, new placement and the educators adjusting to the notion of an autistic child being fully inclusioned in the classroom, with support from the special education department. The school balked at the idea of inclusionment, stating that this placement was not an appropriate fit for Kim's needs. After Kim showed she could be an equal member of the class* she won over their hearts and their minds.

For more information, refer to "The Girl Who Spoke With Pictures," By Eileen Miller, Jessica Kingsley Pub. 2008 pgs. 102-104

All in all, I was very pleased with the way things were progressing. And then, from out of the blue, something came along that broadsided all of us. No one could have seen it coming, and we were clueless as to the cause.

The date was Wednesday, February 9. Kim walked happily into class like any ordinary day. I waved goodbye and headed for home across the street. About an hour and a half later, I received a call that Kim was not feeling well and needed to come home. Mrs. Kellen, the classroom assistant, had Kim packed up and ready by the time I got there.

Both Mrs. Kellen and teacher, Mrs. Friendly, had remarked about how suddenly her illness had come upon her. They said that when she came in from recess, her eyes were watery, and she looked worried. She told them that she wanted Mom and needed to go home.

After walking Kim to our house, I could hear her stomach gurgling—often a sign of her emotional distress. She was visibly shaken and retreated to her bed, which was totally out of character for her. I was very concerned, but children get sick all the time. I told myself I shouldn't fuss, and she seemed to have recovered completely by the time Marcia came home from school. However, the following morning Kim announced that she was staying home, and whenever I raised the subject of school, tears came to her eyes. Perhaps she was not as well yet as I thought. It was always so difficult to tell if she was sick. She wasn't running a fever. She was not listless. There was no physical sign to tell me what was going on in that body of hers, so thinking it better to err on the side of caution, I kept her home.

The next morning Kim once again said she needed to stay home. By this time I didn't know what to do because she was still so distressed. I phoned the teacher, and we agreed that, because it was Friday, it might be better to wait. We would give her the next two days to get over whatever was causing this, and she could start fresh on Monday.

I asked if they had drastically changed anything in her schedule or the classroom environment, but there was nothing they could think of. Kim seemed to be her regular self all weekend until Sunday night, when John and I broke the news that she would be attending school on Monday. Kim fell apart. She began crying softly to herself and curled up in a fetal position behind John's recliner in the corner of the living room. We tried to coax her to talk to us about what was bothering her, but she only whimpered.

John gave her a slice of cheesecake, her very favorite food, to calm her down, but she fell asleep with the plate balanced on her stomach—the cake barely touched.

Kim did not want to dress herself for school the next morning. I told her I would have to do it myself if she did not. She was apprehensive about going out the door, all the while voicing her objections. With my hand lightly on her back, I propelled her tiny body forward, and as I held her arm, I felt goose-bumps raised so roughly that her skin felt like sandpaper. She was walking like a sleepwalker, stiffly and without purpose.

I coaxed her to the flagpole and then, with much pleading and begging, to the outside corner of the kindergarten wing of the school. The closer we got to Mrs. Friendly's room, the smaller her steps, and sometimes she walked backward, so we lost a bit of ground. It took more than ten minutes to cover ten feet of sidewalk. If I hadn't been so worried, I would have been extremely cross with her.

The bell rang, and all the children rushed to their classrooms. Kim's feet suddenly seemed cemented to the pavement. I tried slipping into one of her favorite characters from the Disney's "Rescuer's" movie. I pretended that I was a mouse in need of help.

"Help me, Kim." I reached out my arms.

She reached back toward me, but her feet were still glued to the ground. I gave up. It was February 14. Valentine's Day. I was disappointed that Kim would miss the party that would be held at the end of the day, but I didn't know what to do, and her classmates were beginning to notice through the window and be distracted. As I began to take Kim away from her classroom, I noticed that her feet were not so heavy.

My friend, Stella, had recently begun her position as a behavioral specialist at our school, so we went to her room. I explained our dilemma. We started to brainstorm, and I phoned the autism specialist, too. With the phone in hand, we tossed out ideas for possible causes of Kim's sudden inability to enter the classroom. It just didn't make sense. All of us were stumped.

The autism specialist, still on the other end of the line, asked if anyone had hurt Kim's feelings. I asked Kim if "a friend had hurt her heart," and she said yes. Even if a friend had actually done or said something to offend her, Kim wouldn't be able to pass on details to us, so how would we ever find out who it was, let alone what was said or done? The autism specialist recommended that all of the children in the classroom be made to apologize to Kim.

Now, everyone knows how difficult it is to get children to say they are sorry even when they *are* in the wrong, so I didn't think it was feasible to make them all apologize when they hadn't done anything. However, by that time I was willing to try almost anything.

Just then, another call came in. She seemed to know me and called me by name although the voice on the line was unfamiliar. I explained that we were having problems with Kim, and she said she had some simple drawings of feelings depicted on a set of cards in her office. Stella ran to get them. We set the cards in front of Kim and instructed her to point to how she was feeling.

At first, I thought she was posturing her hands, but she was actually mimicking the gesture on the "afraid" card. Missing it totally, I kept telling her to put her hands down and point, until Kim started to withdraw and stare.

Stella could tell I was getting tense and frustrated, so she told me she would work with Kim while I went home.

Later, Stella called and said that it took a long time, but she did finally walk Kim into the Valentine's party. It was already in progress when she arrived. She made it to the threshold and then dashed in with her head down. I thanked Stella profusely. Finally, we had made it!

However, February 15 was not much better. Kim still was agitated over going to school. We had the same struggles in the morning, but Kim's best friend helped coax her into the room. It still took twenty-five minutes.

Mrs. Kellen and Mrs. Friendly were clearly perplexed. They had searched high and low to find anything out of the ordinary. Then the answer came. Simply. Ever since Kim was able to enter the room, she had been shielding her eyes with her hand as though a bright light were shining. She ducked her head as she moved from one task to another. Then, Mrs. Kellen reminded Kim to put her glue away.

"You'll never get me to the back of the room!" Kim replied, and from where Mrs. Kellen stood, she could see it: a poster of the simplified anatomy of a little boy. It showed a photograph of his head, but his circulatory system (including the heart with its arteries and veins) was illustrated inside the outline of his body. It was obvious that the picture terrified Kim, and right next to this poster was a drawing of the anatomy of the human heart.

When Mrs. Friendly checked her lesson plan book, she saw that she had put the poster up while the children were out to recess on that Wednesday that Kim so suddenly fell ill. The teacher immediately took the poster of the little boy down, but Kim was still visually disturbed over the drawing of the heart. It was interesting that when I asked her if "a friend had hurt her heart," she said yes. The fact that it literally dealt with a picture of a heart is intriguing.

Kim didn't seem to hold anyone responsible for the appearance of the posters, but she felt that the security of the environment had been breached, and she had no idea when or where other terrifying things might suddenly pop up in the classroom again. The enemy, for Kim, was unpredictability. This particular incident brought home to the teachers and staff at school, the importance of writing down observations, to look for the reason behind behavior, and that visual images can have a disturbing impact.

Mrs. Kellen checked the paper assignments for troubling images such as clowns, drawings of x-rays, faces on inanimate objects, or anything that she could see that might cause problems, and Kim began to understand that she had some control and seek out help in removing any upsetting objects from her paper.

About a week after what was referred to as "the poster incident" at school, I received a call from Mrs. Friendly. She was so excited! All the pieces of this child had come together in her mind. She explained how she finally really saw that Kim was not willful, but she was reactionary to her environment and that everything depended on communication. Kim was like a computer. A person had to know how to enter the information as well as to understand how to access it—to get the details out. Sometimes it required the same echolalic phrase or verbage and intonation to gain access, a key to unlocking what was inside Kim's thought processes. She also learned that whatever happened at school carried over into our home life and whatever happened at home, affected school. We had to work together to create consistency in both environments and communicate any changes or unusual circumstances which could alter her behavior. By doing so, we could channel her mind and energy towards learning.

Word spread around the school of the autistic girl who couldn't enter the classroom and of the teacher and the assistant who put the puzzle together. They no longer had to work at "pulling" Kim into the class flow. It was now just a natural part of their teaching skills, and never again would I receive reports of Kim being "in her own little world." Instead, I read journal entries which gave insights into strategies for teaching and observations to help in reinforcing Kim's speech and social interactions. The more detail that was included in the journal, the more support our family could give to their efforts. For example, giving visual cues was a vital part of cutting through the overwhelming of auditory information, especially if Kim was in a crowded room. Imagine being in a classroom. The teacher is talking to a table of students, an assistant is talking to a child, classmates are chatting to one another. Which person should you tune into? Where is the relevant information for you? How can other people help you sort out what is important information and what is not? Whenever I was accompanying Kim in a setting, I would sign the word listen, by holding the letter "L" near my ear and then pointing to the person who she should attend to. This small action was so important to direct her attention to the vital information, a physical cue to cut through the vast information bombarding her senses. This was a way for her to visually cue into what was the information she should be listening for, the same information that her peers naturally keyed into. Advising the teacher that giving last minute instructions or reminders just after the bell rings, while bodies are shifting and scuffling, is like trying to listen to breaking news over a Public Address system during a stampede. Little tips went a long way in transforming Kim from a child who was frustrated by her environment to a sweet girl, who wanted to attend school and learn like everyone else.

Mrs. Friendly began stapling a photocopy of her lesson plan for the upcoming week in the journal so that I could support the learning goals at home. As time wore on, the teachers could anticipate regressions or learning spurts (time periods of keen perception) by interpreting a developing pattern from the journal entries. Mrs Kellen recorded her thoughts and concerns in the journal as well as writing down information for me. She really understood the purpose of the journal: to write down ideas, record observations, ask questions of the family and of herself. It was more of a method of thinking out loud, she didn't expect us to have answers for all the questions. I appreciated the fact that she didn't compare Kim's skills or development to the other children. Instead, she looked at Kim and asked, "Where do we want Kim to be? How can we get her there? What do we want Kim to be able to do? How can we enable her to do it?"

The journal evolved into an in more versatile document. When it came time to write goals in the Individual Education Program (IEP), we gathered a list from the journal and then prioritized them in order of importance. Documentation is crucial because if the child shows need of more services or if there is a disagreement regarding appropriate placement, services or staffing, the journal can be reviewed to see if the changes are warranted. In this regard it became a powerful document. Because budgets for the school had been slashed, the amount of observation time for the autism specialist to have in the classroom was minimized as well as consultation with parents and teacher. The problem was solved by the autism specialist reading the daily notes, then writing her recommendations regarding ideas on troubleshooting. The specialist could also see the practically seamless teamwork that is so vital in the process of maintaining continuity on all environments.

Samples of Journal Entries:

**Things you need to know:*
- *Kim's fears are pictures of x-rays or cut-aways of anatomy and pictures of bees/wasps*
- *She is slowly overcoming her dread of clowns.*
- *The color red means "hot."*

- *Stickers are very motivational, and she thrives with positive verbal along with visual reinforcement.*
- *When she jumps up and down, flapping her arms, she is extremely pleased.*
- *She now wants to know the names of everything she sees, so do not assume that she knows the names of common items.*

Thank you,
Eileen

Educators had very little time to get to know my daughter. It took me years of careful observation to become familiar with my own child. For them to take the time, it would be an expensive and almost impossible task. I jotted down what I felt they needed to know in small short notes. They needed to know that if she did something unusual, how to interpret what she meant. Kim was constantly misunderstood because others lacked the reference or context where she was coming from. I didn't give it to them all at once, I couldn't expect them to wade through pages and pages. It was easier to give them a short paragraph to digest every day.

Her first week of kindergarten was quite a testing ground for both parent and educator. I gave them my best shot at writing a small note to clue them into the direction in which Kim's mind was leading:

Sept. 6 *KINDERGARTEN:*

Kim preferred that I whisper as we reviewed her daily classroom schedule. She is familiar with the symbols and their meanings except for "line up." She has been echoing phrases from "The Great Pumpkin" from Charles Shultz comic strip, Peanuts. She particularly likes Lucy's line where she says, "I'll slug you." She does not mean these words. She just likes the sound of them.

Something helpful to remember: Look for the <u>reason </u>behind the behavior. Have a good day!

Eileen

The teachers did their best to communicate with the journal at this time, but it was so new to them in their experience, they were trying to find their way. They mentioned that she had yelled something that sounded like, "You're a butt!" I found that hard to believe. Knowing and having documented her limited vocabulary, I didn't doubt that she said something, but it wasn't that word. This is why I dutifully logged Kim's phrases, obsession, and words because teachers would then have a clue as to what she was saying. Since she had never used swear words before and our family not using profanity or inappropriate language, odds were quite small that she would say anything of that nature. I later discovered, after listening to her, that she was saying Lucy's line in an (echolalic manner) from a "Peanuts" cartoon, "You blockhead." Her spoken language was quite garbled because she was new at speaking words, she had trouble annunciating and therefore it was not clear what she had uttered. The fact that they had not had access to Kim around the clock, caused them to believe that she was either swearing at them or being mean and disrespectful. They didn't realize that she was living or play acting in the role of a cartoon character. At first they were a little dubious to accept this concept as an explanation for her words, after all, many parents defend their children's actions, even if they are wrong. The situation came about again a few months later, when the assistant came to work with her in the classroom on speech therapy. Kim tossed her hair and turned her back on the therapist who was absolutely bewildered. Knowing Kim's obsession at the time, I explained to the therapist that she was being treated with distain, not because she was not liked or accepted, but because she was an alligator villain in the current cartoon movie obsession. As soon as I apprised the educators on the frame of reference in Kim's mind, they were better equipped to handle a child with such a dramatic imagination. Since Kim had developed her talent in art by this time, her drawings came to the rescue to bolster my claim regarding the origin of her behavior. This is why I refer to Kim as one small but significant bridge between the verbal and nonverbal worlds. To me, this is a huge step to realize the behavior that we as parents, teachers and society are reading is skewed. We are interpreting it from our position whereas we should take a clue and examine each individual from the familial microcosm in which the autistic individual is exposed. She was misunderstood for her actions for quite some time until she could physically draw out a context that we could relate to, on paper. In hindsight, I could have sent the videotape of the cartoons to the school for them to view so that they could copy down bits of language to prompt Kim into speaking. It would have been a valuable creative teaching tool at the time. We did this at home as a way to relate to Kim and get her to respond to us, I just didn't think that it was feasible for the teacher or assistant to spend their spare time learning about one child.

Sept. 20 KINDERGARTEN

Kim looked like she didn't feel well today. Didn't want to do her letter "T" paper and wrote Marcia's name at the top. After I cut off the picture (a tree with a smiling face), she was fine, so I must

*remember to do that on penmanship papers that have pictures of
inanimate objects with faces.*

Mrs. Kellen

This was an important notation showing that the education staff took Kim's
genuine concerns over images in earnest. Without the documentation of the
poster incident in the journal, any problems I raised in connection with her
inability to attend class, would not have been taken seriously.

Kim's classroom assistant was very astute in her observations and often
posed thought provoking questions:

***Sept. 9 FIRST GRADE**
*How can we help Kim focus on the front of the room? Is she being
pulled in enough? Kim had a lot of problems today with a reading
comprehension test. The teacher read a story and then asked questions.
Kim wanted to draw a picture instead. I couldn't pull her in...also drew
a picture that I don't think was on topic for Math, which was about
friends sharing cookies.*

Mrs. Kellen

I was not surprised to read this entry. For an autistic person who processes
information visually, a story read aloud isn't processed. To take an oral test
on a subject of information given auditorily puts this individual at a great
disadvantage because there is nothing visual to lock in their attention. It was
very difficult for Kim to convert the auditory information into information
she could "see." To hear without seeing would be very frustrating for her. It
was no wonder that she just sat silently drawing a picture.

***Sept. 29 FIRST GRADE**
*Kim had a pretty good day today. She went with the new girl and me to
tour the school while the other kids rearranged their desks (being aware
that the sound of the children moving their desks is uncomfortable for
Kim). When we started out the door, she commented on how "dirty"
it was outside. I talked to her about the leaves falling and why it was
"dirty," but what an interesting observation. She's right, Fall is messy,
ha!*

Mrs. Kellen

Staff making notes about simple actions like moving desks was vital because if Kim were overwhelmed with sound during the day, the upsetness could carry over into the night. The assistant, after having a small inservice/ training, could spot what problems could arise from simple actions. She eliminated the concern knowing that she could head off the problem and be proactive realizing it was much easier to avoid the irritant than to deal with the fall out afterwards. By recording in the diary of what went on in Kim's day often gave us a reason to attribute to her behavior when she was at home and to adjust accordingly.

Oct. 25 FIRST GRADE

A little girl joined our group today. We had her come to the back of the room and started our lesson as usual. All of a sudden Kim won't do the work...and I'm thinking, "What's going on?" Then Kim is looking at the little girl, and it dawns on me that this is something different. Sooo, I acknowledged, "Yes, I'm sorry, Kim. Jenny is in our group now, too," and we counted boys, and we counted girls, and life was fine!

Mrs. Kellen

The aide didn't just discount Kim's behavior as being autistic or willful, she looked for the reason behind the behavior. She could have brushed it off, although deep down she knew that if Kim reacted to something, it must be important. The assistant found a quick fix and moved on with the lesson with very little disruption.

Nov. 4 FIRST GRADE

Kim was distracted today and kind of distant but I was easily able to pull her back in. I will say that there have been a lot of physical changes in our classroom:

- *We have tables instead of desks, so Kim sits with four other kids.*
- *Her schedule is on my desk instead of hers.*
- *Reading group is now done at a rectangular table at the back of the room.*
- *Recess is now in the corridors instead of the playground because of foul weather.*
- *Supplies are kept at the back of the classroom due to no desks.*

Anyway, this in addition to Halloween, I know is very hard.

Mrs. Kellen

Mrs. Kellen noted the changes in the physical school environment (tables instead of desks), anticipated changes in routine (Halloween holiday), and the fact that the educators recognized that this would be challenging for Kim.

Dec. 8 FIRST GRADE

I decided to jot down a couple of things while on my break...Kim was really out of sorts with everything yesterday. Talking out, wanting to be the one called on, not being cooperative. You know the mood, ha! However, she was <u>much</u> better today! I think the idea of being pulled out to another room for Math kind of threw her.

The last couple of days, if I didn't know Kim and information on autism, I would swear Kim was being deliberately naughty. However, since I know her, she's probably reacting to changes in seasons <u>and</u> in changes we've put in her day. Like I said, today <u>was</u> better. I've built in a Math magnet for her schedule since the time flip-flops between before and after recess.

There is a new girl whose presence seems to upset Kim a little. She came at almost exactly the same time another little girl moved away. They're both blonde-haired and blue-eyed, and she even sits in the same spot as the other girl. I think it's all a little confusing.
Mrs. Kellen

They were more empathetic and understanding of Kim's more autistic moments as well as being supportive in her triumphs.

March 10 FIRST GRADE

...In order to relieve a little monotony, we've been counting, one student at a time... Anyway, I have them count like that instead of all together. Kim gets stuck and won't participate unless she gets to count 6 or 16 or 26. I've tried to avoid this problem by arranging it so that the number at her turn will be 6 or...

The child who moved out of local area at the first of the year has moved back. She came today. Kim was really happy and handled the change fine. I hope this will help her with the moving thing (friends moving in and out of different communities.) I would hope it would help her to see that people don't vanish.
Mrs. Kellen

A very sharp observation! Kim had a problem with understanding time and space. People popped into her circle of life and then vanished. Because no one thought to sit down and talk to her about the fact that children often move to another school or even out of the community. It was so confusing and disorienting.

March 31 *FIRST GRADE*

...Kim still wants to read only certain words, and I told her that everyone just reads the words as they come, otherwise the reading would be too scattered and disruptive. I usually say that if she doesn't want that word, I'll just call on someone else. Kim reads it then.

Mrs. Kellen

May 5 *SECOND **GRADE***

...I've noticed that Kim has been more withdrawn the last couple of weeks. I'm assuming end- of-the-year has a lot to do with that. All the kids are sensing it, but I'm sure it must be harder for Kim. The last day of school will just be fun and games. Also, I'm sure the kids will help take down the room decorations in the classroom. All of this will be hard for her, so you might want to start preparing her, however you feel best, to help her handle it. (Cont'd)

If you think of something we've forgotten, let me know.

Mrs. Kellen

Mrs. Kellen was familiar with the end of the year procedures in the classroom and gave us a list of activities that we should be aware of, such as field trips, picnics, and things the children would be bringing home, so we could properly prepare Kim. At one point, Kim began to bite her arm in an abusive way. The assistant took the time to take her student aside to talk about the end of the year activities, how that might make her feel and acknowledged that it was a difficult time. Without making Kim feel strange, she discussed how the bite marks in the skin was the body's way of letting her know that it didn't like to be hurt. It helped turn Kim's attention to what she was doing to her own body.

In the 3rd grade classroom, the assignment was to teach the children to refine their writing skills. They were to write a simple rough draft. Then revise it to a much neater copy. For a person with autism, the task was redundant and confusing. Kim, ever the perfectionist felt that she had accomplished task the first time.

When she was learning to spell some years earlier, she was most disturbed when I was guiding her one letter at a time. Some letters as you well know are repeated in a word. This did not compute in Kim's mind, and heaven forbid if there was a double vowel or consonant! Trying to convey the reason with a partially verbal, frustrated, child on the verge of a tantrum, that more than one letter repeats in a word is a challenge.

You can imagine the bewilderment and frustration when she had complied with the assignment given, only to find out that the teachers wanted her to repeat the act of writing the same story on another piece of paper. She felt that she had spelled, punctuated and written the story to her satisfaction. Why in the world would she want to do it again? In her eyes it was perfect and there was no reason for her to do the same exercise. She completed it, time to move on. But the teachers wouldn't move on, they wanted her to write the same assignment over. Even as this notation was being recorded in the journal, teacher and assistant were problem solving:

Nov. 8 THIRD GRADE

...Kim balked at doing a "rewrite" of a writing assignment today. Mrs. Kellen tried to reason with her, but she was still saying "no" ten minutes into the assignment. We both discussed with her the fact that unfinished work will be done this afternoon in Study Hall. She began to rewrite the assignment then. Now, I've noticed she is writing a different story, still refusing to edit and re-write. Mrs. Kellen, again, is trying to negotiate.

Note:

She finally finished the original letter but changed "Hawaii" to "Bahamas" because "there are too many coconuts in Hawaii."

> *Here is the pattern:*
> *Anger*
> *Refusal to comply*
> *Writing sloppily*
> *Eventual compliance with much prompting.*

Compliance always comes with a twist (on her terms)

We asked why she didn't like to do this. She said "It's not fair." We pointed out that the others in the class are doing the same assignment. We know that she definitely <u>doesn't</u> want to save this for study hall.
*   Mrs. Kellen*

The assistant wrote out the steps of the behavior that Kim was exhibiting which was important to record so that they could recognize what triggered the oncoming behavior. They studied the process that Kim was going through then they came up with a plan:

Nov. 12 THIRD GRADE

Just a note to mention what we discussed this morning. We brainstormed regarding the sloppy copy versus finished product activity. Will try:

> *(1) Telling Kim to compare the corrections made by the teacher to the spell check on the computer. If that doesn't work,*
>
> *(2) Put sticky notes on top of her sloppy copy or on her desk listing the steps to correcting her paper to make her understand that her first copy is only half of the completed project. The problem with this particular road block is that a re-write is not required on every paper or even on a paper every week. The inconsistency makes it tough to reinforce. Wish us luck?*
>
> *Mrs. Kellen*

All of us could learn from Mrs. Kellen. She understood autism so well. She knew that once Kim began to understand about doing a "sloppy copy" and a finished copy, that her little student might generalize the idea and begin to apply that to all of her homework.

The reason that I posted many of her observations was that I wanted to have a model of how to properly write journal entries. The document started out as a type of diary of Kim's behavior, body rhythms, sleep and learning patterns. It then evolved into a document of communication between home and school. It served as a record that could be reviewed to save time and precious money resources by becoming a time saving tool for professionals. Lastly, it provided facts to be reviewed regarding to progress towards goals. We were able to spot patterns of behavior to support the positive and down play the negative. In one instance, we were able to pin point an interest of Kim's that began to grow into an obsession. I am of the opinion, the way deal with obsessions is to saturate and satiate Kim's interest until she became satisfied as long as it does not hurt her or anyone else and is not dangerous. In this particular case, she was obsessed with a game that the children played during "free time." It had to do with pieces of round glass that were an amber color. She referred to them as the "golden stones." Whatever it was about the game, the reflection of light off of the glassy rock, the smoothness in texture, the lovely color, she could think of nothing else. I suggested to the teacher that she send the game home with Kim so that we as a family could play it continually throughout the course of a week. She could play the game, look at the pieces to suit her interest and finally get rid of the unknown. I must admit, playing the game was a little addictive to me as well. After looking at the game and playing it, Kim revealed to me the charm of it all was the glassy reflective colorful stones. We went to the store, bought some colorful glass aquarium rocks and took the game back to school. I let her take a couple of the small rocks in her pocket so that she could have them at any time and it was not forbidden. The obsession passed, she no longer needed to carry the stones with her. We had mowed down the distraction of such an alluring obsession so that Kim could focus on the important information such as school work.

- Sensitizing Kim to the realization she can hurt her body.
- Making her aware of the speaker in the room by cueing her into the person by signing "listen" next to the ear and pointing.
- Desensitizing her to upsetting images or removing drawings entirely from her homework
- Writing down the context of her thoughts and imaginations
- Clueing teachers and therapists to her pattern of speech-what was present and not present- using our knowledge to build upon.
- Communicating and being informed about the environment and subjects that Kim was exposed so that home and school could provide continuity in routine and daily living
- Recording what circumstances/stimulus's brought about the need for speech, what circumstances caused favorable and unfavorable reactions.
- Recording observations of patterns of behavior: regressions, learning breakthroughs and the causes for non compliance.

I'm sure that there are more discoveries to be made in the course of your autism journey. These are some examples of just a few learning opportunities that I had the honor of sharing with educators as we discovered and unlocked the inner workings of Kim's mind. The journal is driven by the quest for knowledge and discovery, not an ego centric need to validate or excuse the behavior of an autistic child.

Chapter 5

Mind, Body and Spirit

The Human Body

The human body and how it works in conjunction with the mind is utterly fascinating. Of course we take for granted that our minds tell our bodies how to move through space, coordinating muscles, our skin detecting the slightest pressure or temperature change. It wasn't until I was raising my autistic daughter that I became so painfully aware of what kind of consequences from the happenings in everyday life would have on her body. If it wasn't for the journal, we would not have been able to isolate the "cause and effect" connection between Kim's mind and the reaction of her body.

In the Beginning

Since birth, she always had very sensitive skin. At first it was because she held her neck so tightly that it formed a wrinkle in the base of the neck area. No air could get circulate there and she began to develop sores. I used baby oil twice a day to clean the skin which was the only thing that made a difference. But her skin seemed to be always bumpy.

As she grew older as a toddler, the problem appeared to sort itself out, so I didn't dwell on the issue and moved on. However, from time to time, small red bumps would appear at the base of her neck and her trunk. I discounted them as a random rash, strange things that seemed to always happen so I had an explanation for everything. There was one particular incident involving my husband's family staying in our home for a visit. The mysterious red rash emerged again. What was it? I noted in the spiral bound journal. Mary wrote back, after consulting the timeline in the writing, and suggested that perhaps it might be the result the stimulation of all of our guests. I thought that might be a bit of a stretch, the notion that having different people in the house could possibly affect her body that way. After the company had left, the breakout on Kim's skin left as quickly as it came. Thinking back, there was much excitement (sensory information) going on in our house, more bodies sharing a confined habitat (space), the expressive pitch of our voices (auditory), continual hugging (tactile). For a person who is sensory sensitive, it was a circuit just waiting to overload. When her mind was overwhelmed and the stimulation level could not be self regulated, something had to give, and it manifested itself in the way of breaking out on her skin. Then, as now, I monitor the stimulation just as a person with insulin issues monitors their blood levels. Ever watchful of signs of overstimulation, stress and anxiety, I turn to the best source of information.

This is when I learned to listen to Kim's body.

Kim Falls Down

Most children fall down all the time, but Kim was blessed with an incredible sense of balance and judgment of space. She did not ever fall down, stub her toe, or trip. Ever constantly in motion whether it was leaping from couch to chair or galloping in a circle in the middle of the floor, I was always struck by her coordination at such an early age. I know this sounds incredibly unusual, but she was careful with her body. Because of this, when she fell down on the pavement of the playground while playing kick-ball during third grade, it unnerved her quite a bit. She had never really fallen down before. She scraped her cheek and there were two bumps on her head. She had obviously broken her fall with her hands as she had scratches on her palms. A couple of classmates escorted her to the office for band-aids and reassurances, and although shaken up, she functioned appropriately in class.

When one of the secretaries in the office phoned at 10:10 a.m. to notify us that Kim had bumped her head, I was not home to answer the call. The teacher called about 45 minutes later requesting a parent to come over to the school to give tender loving care. Finally, when I arrived home at noon, Mrs. Kellen called and said that Kim was sick.

I arrived there to find Kim anxious to go home, and as soon as we stepped through the door at home, she threw up on the floor and began to appear drowsy. I phoned the school to find out what happened, but no adult had really seen her hit the ground. I tried to explain that I wasn't mad or upset, but I really needed to know how she hit, so I could relay the information to a doctor if necessary. It seemed to take a long time to find someone who witnessed her accident, and then, the only thing they could get out of the children was that they said they didn't see her hit her head.

It was frustrating to say the least, to try to figure out what had happened with no one who saw and Kim unable to tell us. She was totally silent— withdrawn and spacey. Staring straight ahead, not taking in the objects in the room, it was almost like one of her seizures, I was getting scared.

John, who was working on patrol, came by the house and checked her eyes. The pupils were normal. Kim was barely responding to questions, and I kept poking her to make sure she wasn't having seizures. Then my mother dropped in unexpectedly and had a toy for Kim. Kim showed no interest at all.

I began to run a bath. She viewed her wound in the mirror with a lack of expression, but then, as she sat in the warm water, she began to relax. This longtime cue that we "built in" to our strategies for calming down was working.

In the prior year, John and I had noticed that Kim seemed to be very suggestive, and highly influenced with snappy slogans. She had to have Kentucky Fried Chicken™ because on the commercial their motto was, "We Do Chicken Right." The same type thing happened when Dominos Pizza™ came up with a winner, "It's Gotta Be-Gotta Be Dominos." Those types of advertisements soaked in and lodged in her brain to the point that whenever we had chicken or pizza, according to Kim, it had to be those restaurants. We figured since the suggestions of such things were so effective, that we should use it to our advantage. We patterned our ideas after this type of system by telling her that when she was tense, that she should have a bath. We implanted the words into her mind, using phrases like, "The bath will relax you." or "You always feel better when you soak in a bath." Sometimes we used hot chocolate, which "it will make you sleepy," although we were very reluctant to utilize a food in our strategy.

She was much more herself after her soak in regards to the school incident. There were no seizures as a result of this fall. Not at any time did she express the physical feeling of soreness or pain from the wound hurting. Days and weeks after the accident, Kim looked at her wound in the mirror, and as it started to heal, she grew more and more lighthearted, until finally, the scrape was all gone. Because she never really experienced a physical wound or healing before, Kim must have thought the large scrape mark would be on her face for the rest of her life. The word Autism means "self" or "self aware." It only stands to reason that she was acutely cognizant of the position of her body in conjunction with the objects in the room and the distance between. The thing that upset my daughter the most was the fact that what happened was unexpected, it was a surprise, she had not been prepared for it. She did not like any appearance of having made a mistake, any mistake. The wound was almost an outward signal to everyone that she had been imperfect. Secondly, she could not remove the wound from her face.

Kim was 4 years old, when she burned herself on the hand, she tried to remove the blisters immediately by clawing at her hand. I had to restrain her for hours from trying to remove the wounds. With her body on my lap facing outward, both of my hands firmly gripping her arms, holding them as far away from each other as possible. If I relaxed, she took advantage and began to thrash about in an attempt to scratch her hand. I believe that she thought that if she could remove the physical aspect of the burn that it would go away.

The same kind of circumstances occurred as a result of the game incident at school. She just could not understand the cause and effect of any type of injury. Kim was more disturbed by having to wear the badge of a war wound. She became physically ill from the abruptness of the event, not necessarily the impact of being hurt.

The Field Trip

Whenever there was a field trip, teachers tried to prepare the students with material over which they would be tested by giving a pre-test, and they instructed the children to be on their best behavior. It was a way for the teacher to focus the students on the information they were expected to learn on that particular field trip and to give them enough knowledge about the subject to enable them to ask intelligent questions.

Early in the school year, a field trip was announced for Kim's fourth grade class. The subject of the pre-test was "You and the Law." The trip was announced weeks in advance so that the children had plenty of opportunity to mind or mend their behavior and to soak up some of the information that was to prepare them for the trip. This was a good strategy for many of the children, but for Kim, it was a torturous wait.

The "test" was quite easy for anyone who read the literature provided, and the students were given plenty of opportunity to pass it, but they had been told that if they didn't pass, they would not be allowed to go on the field tip. Also, anyone not obeying the day-to-day rules would not be eligible to go. The anticipation was just too much for Kim. Students often have to be constantly reminded of their duty to be responsible for their actions, but Kim took these reminders directly to heart; it caused her the following anxiety:

Oct. 1

I found the journal under a scroll (7) notebook pages long. Last night Kim was obsessed with owning a health spa. She was driven to write down the names of all the machines she would need in her health club. She draped the list (scroll) over the couch because she was proud of it and wanted us to see it when we woke up. She was up late last night. What set her off was the fact that she had some homework that was due Friday, and she did not know what it was, but she was all in a tizzy about it. We looked. It wasn't written in the homework notebook. Marcia surmised that it might be the "You and The Law" test. Kim, all upset, had to calm down with the TV.

Eileen

Oct. 2

After school, Kim was extremely unfocused. She couldn't settle down to do her homework. She is usually enthusiastic and gets it done right away without prompting.

She stayed up late last night very agitated. Finally, I put her fuzzy blanket into the dryer to warm it up, then bundled her. She finally relaxed and became drowsy.

Eileen

After two days with no response, I called Mrs. James at school. She had been out of town and had been unable to respond. She had been looking over the last couple of day's notations in the journal, and was trying to come up with a reasonable explanation for the behaviors and rashes. At the time we didn't know for sure that the "You and The Law" test was causing all the problems. Together we wondered what the exact stressor was and how we could modify Kim's behavior.

Oct. 7

Kim was unfocused and hyperactive on Friday, Saturday, and Sunday. We redirected her attention to books and videos. On Sunday, she developed a rash on the collarbone. It grew worse by the hour, creeping up her neck. (Unusual. It often starts on her chest and gravitates down.) We felt it was a result of change in her schedule (Open House at school). The event came and went. At first, she was reluctant to go to the school because of the number of people there, but once there, she was fine.

This evening she was very distressed about "The Law" test. She was fretting and crying. John and I diverted her attention. I've noticed some neck scratching.

Eileen

Oct. 8

...She also told me she was worried about "The Law" test, but I tried to let her know that I would help her pass the test and that she would be able to go.

Mrs. James

Oct. 10

> *She was up until 12:00 last night. Bouncing, flapping, pacing, taking time to look at her reflection in the window.*
>
> Eileen

I finally phoned Mrs. James at home and asked what we could do about this situation. I didn't like to ask for special favors for Kim, but she needed to be reassured that she would indeed pass the test and be able to attend the field trip. The question of whether or not she would pass the test was just too much for her to bear.

Mrs. James graciously offered to make sure that Kim had enough questions answered correctly to make it to the event. After all, the point of the test was not to cause stress and anxiety, it was to give the children information to consider and absorb while they were on the trip.

Oct. 13

> *When Kim came through the door Friday, there was a notable difference. There has been no more scratching and no more outbreaks of the rash. She went to bed at 8:30 that night. There was no more excessive jumping and flapping. I think it's safe to say that it was the "You and the Law" test that brought it on. Thank you for your help and understanding. Her passing meant we would have a good weekend.*
>
> Eileen

The teacher and I worked together to isolate the cause of the behavior. I could rule out any out of the ordinary changes in her home environment, routine, etc. The teacher considered the same as well, leaving the only conclusion being the "You and the Law" test. By using the journal for communication, observation and confirmation, we took all of the variables out of the question and came up with the solution. By giving the test to Kim early, we headed off a needless crisis and saved the wear and tear on her body.

Pending test

By the time high school rolled around, I almost had this mind/body thing down to a science. Unfortunately, we no longer kept a journal that went back and forth from home to school. The school day broken down into six different segments of time, six different teachers, environments, groups of classmates, keeping track by the way of written journal would have been difficult. The advent of email was a blessing. I could quickly shoot off messages of information for the 10th grade teachers that would be helpful when working with Kim such as upcoming holidays, concepts that were difficult, current obsessions as well as trouble shooting concerns.

The year was going quite well when I noticed scratches on her arms. She wasn't particularly delicate when she clawed at her skin so the marks were conspicuous. I asked her why she was scratching and she stated that she didn't know, but I knew. I started to ask her pointed questions such as, "Is there a project that was due?" "Did a teacher promise you something?" "A field trip coming up?" She answered no to each question. For the next few days, I observed more scratching even deeper into the skin. Knowing what this meant after having experienced the "You and the Law" test from years prior, I picked up the phone and asked to be connected to each teacher in turn. I asked them without hesitation, if they had anything, "pending." Any project that was postponed or waiting. The teachers said that everything was fine, that Kim turned her work in on time as always. I pressed them once more, particularly stressing the word, "pending." I knew to them I was talking in circles. Because they had so little time and so many students, they did not get to know me that well, and did not know how I worked nor how tuned into Kim that I was through my observations. Her physical education teacher said that he had noticed Kim scratching in gym class and assumed there must be a medical reason. A week went by and no improvement. She seemed to suffer, but then again, Thanksgiving and Christmas holidays were coming up. One day Kim came home from school and mentioned that she had a substitute teacher for the last several weeks in biology class. I immediately phoned the school to talk to the teacher. I asked her if she knew of any class project, a test…that could be waiting. She promptly replied that there was a test that was supposed to have been administered by the teacher but he was called away suddenly for paternity leave. He had decided that she should not give the test, that he would do it when he came back. Of course, no one knew exactly when that would be. Meanwhile, I told Kim to hang in there, none of the teachers understood how difficult it was for her to wait for something to happen nor the toll it took on her body. Finally the day came when she could purge her being on the test and finally unload that burden. She immediately stopped scratching and life continued. Thanks to the observations in previous years, we were able to pinpoint the source of the problem.

Novocain and the Dentist

It was her junior year of high school when she had the braces on her teeth removed. I took Kim to her dentist for a simple procedure of removing some gum tissue. She had the utmost faith and trust in this dentist who always took such great care and forethought to treat his autistic patient. He had assured me that only cauterizing and Novocain were involved. She didn't appear to be nervous. I sat in the waiting room glancing at a magazine when suddenly she appeared in front of me, apparently ready to go home. Something was different about her demeanor, she was spacey, almost non-responsive. I was concerned that I was witnessing the beginning of a seizure. I asked her if she was alright, she replied yes, but she wanted to go home. I handed her the keys and hung back to talk to the nurse. I asked if the procedure went well and received a response to the affirmative. I still didn't feel reassured. Meanwhile, Kim had made her way to the car. She was extremely unsteady on her feet. A police officer, who was a friend of the dentist, pulled into the driveway and came in. He remarked about how wobbly Kim was walking out to the car, that he said as a trained observer, he would have claimed she was drunk! By the time I jogged to the car, she was like a stiff doll. I kept asking her questions as I drove home, trying to assess her condition. She was shaking uncontrollably as though she were going into shock and remarked that she couldn't breathe, stating that her heart was beating. I wanted to turn around and go back to the dentist, but I thought it might be best to get her home in John's care and double back to find out what happened. Because of Kim's history of not being able to express adequately how she feels physically and knowing that her mental state is equally important. Again, I had to assess; Was this a type of reaction to the Novocain given, the perceived trauma of the event, was it physical or mental? Was her mental state having an effect on her physical well being? I had to know which system I was dealing with so that I would know where to start. This is a great example of, "just because a person can express themselves verbally, they might not be able to communicate what they are experiencing."

Pain

The notion of physical pain has always been interesting with Kim. She has banged her head on the floor in frustration with no regard to how it felt and yet when a fingernail inadvertently left a white mark path on her skin, she cried out and carried on about excruciating pain. It was puzzling for me, never having met anyone who had such a skewed sense to the feeling of being hurt. Up until the time that she was to have braces put on her teeth, we had not once given pain medication, over the counter or prescription, to Kim. Our oldest daughter, Marcia, had the experience of wearing braces so we were not new to the idea that this could be painful. The day the braces were put on her teeth, we were not sure how pain would register in her brain. Would she go mad with over sensitivity to the sensation of aching and have to have them removed? Or would it be a non issue altogether? Asking Kim about

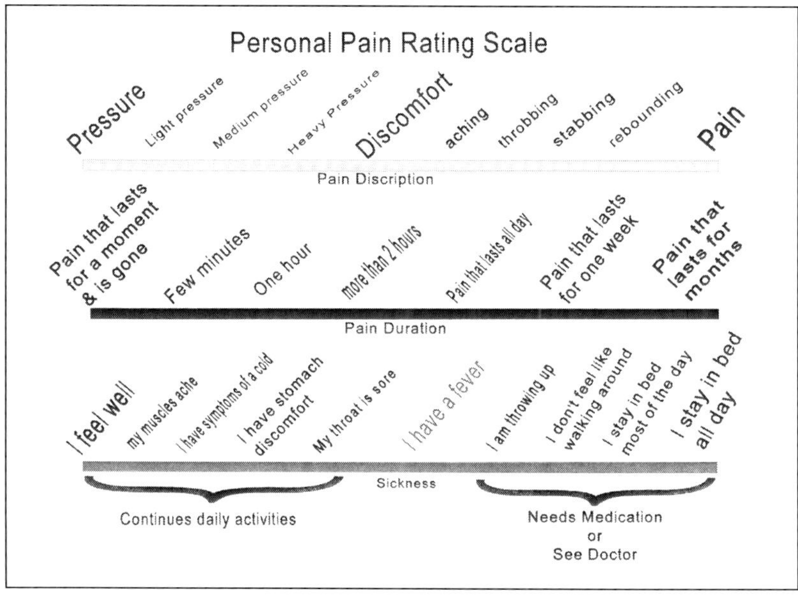

Figure 1.

her comfort level was not the best way to attain information. She needed a simplified way to get the information out in an external method so that others could evaluate her level of wellness. In order for her to show me how she felt, I developed a personal pain/wellness rating scale. Fig.1

By asking as few questions as possible, because any number of inquiries can be overwhelming and frustrating, I had her point to the appropriate place on the scale. Of course, this wasn't necessarily scientific; I developed it to fit Kim's needs. It wouldn't have worked if she had never had the feeling of being sick before, or ever having experienced pain. Up to this point in time, she had been physically ill and experienced physical pain (cause by a real source) only a few instances in her whole life. She needed a frame of reference and since getting braces was the first time that she ever had physical pain with a very specific cause and effect element, she could equate the pain with the tightening of the braces. She learned that some pain is more intense than other sensations, there is a difference between pressure and pain and that pain has a length or time of duration. There is also a quality to pain whether it is sharp or dull, stabbing or squeezing, constant or temporary. All of these issues about the facets of pain have to be defined in order to get a clear picture of what another individual is experiencing and if appropriate, treatment to begin.

Spirit

I believe in the power of prayer. Not just because of the way I was raised to believe in my faith and religion, but because of the essential part it all plays in my life. For me, there is an irrefutable connection between the mind, body and spirit and when attending to one part of an autistic individual, we should address them all. Kim was functionally nonverbal for years with no established communication system, I prayed for her. I poured myself, my energy into asking for wisdom, for help, and if I couldn't teach her, I asked God who created her to teach her heart. There were many parts to my prayers throughout the years. I never asked for her to be healed of autism or for her to be "normal." What I truly wanted was a common ground where we could meet and exist in the same moment, in the same context. When I mention that fact, it means that I wanted her to be able to be with me joining in the same activity with her body and her mind. Have you ever been in a moment where you wanted to turn to someone who was there and have a connection by shared experience? Many times I was pulled away from an activity that I wanted us to join in because she couldn't focus, was too overwhelmed, or didn't understand the intent and was frightened. We were either separated from the activity or Kim had to be removed from me to another room while I attended to what I needed to do. I wanted to share the enjoyment of eating something scrumptious, the sadness of missing something or someone, perhaps just a smile of recognition.

After continual praying I noticed that our situation became better. It was so gradual; it could have been attributed to the willingness that I had to believe. After awhile others seemed to notice and acknowledge the changes in Kim.

Of all the strategies that are in this book, this was the most important, the most powerful, the most personal ways of addressing autism.

CHAPTER 6

Building Support Between Parents And Educators

The popularity of the next three chapters will depend largely upon a person's willingness to step back without regard to their own emotions and viewpoint, to examine the issues from all sides.

The experiences in my daily life such as being the wife of a police officer, college instruction in the education field as well as parenting have shaped my philosophy of how we relate with each other. These facets in my life have given me a unique vantage point on building the bridge of communication and support with these groups. Successful relations between parent, educator, physician and law enforcement; hinges upon the willingness to examine the need for improvement. Professionals who believe their program already addresses gaps in communication has only to read the newspaper to see articles written of autistic children being arrested for an extremely minor infraction of noncompliance in the classroom. By the same token, parents who feel that they have a complete knowledge base of autism need to recognize that act of educating society is not enough. The foundation of preparation needs to be laid, not just within the community but in their children as well.

Any person who feels completely satisfied that their program fits all needs or that they know everything about children with autism should stop reading at this point. They have just fallen into a trap of complacency. When the status quo is upheld, there is no need for alteration. This book is about strategies for change. Recognizing what we can do better and being willing to do so is a must.

After talking to parents through the social networking sites on Facebook and Twitter, I feel the urgent need to gather parents and professionals in one room, locking the door after everyone is inside, and announce, "Today we are going to rip the bandage." Have you ever had a child who knew that they needed to have a bandage that covered their wound removed and they knew there was the possibility that it might hurt, so you promised to do it quickly so that the pain might be minimized? In this instance, it means that we are going to look at the problem that has been covered up and even though it may hurt our egos, we can bring the issue out into the airy light of day. It seems that so many could benefit from learning how to work as a team, but often find the process painful.

During all of the years dealing with the public school system, I've witnessed the need for better understanding and communication. There was such a gap between the perception of the parent of an autistic child and the perception of the professional. Today, I want to bring these two groups closer together by talking about support from the perspective of the professional and from the parent. This is what I have learned by firsthand experience. First I would like to start with the parent side of the Education team before I begin addressing the professional Educators portion.

There is nothing like the moment you find your child has a disability. As in most everyone's experience, I've felt the whole gambit of emotions. One that I didn't expect was the fierce defensive reaction whenever there was any criticism toward my child. I will be the first to say that often fire flashes from my eyes, to which Marcia will admonish me with, "Down Killer!" The mother instinct immediately rises up in me to protect and defend. I have to remember to listen before I begin to react and with that intense feeling of the need to respond, to not overwhelm the other person. I noticed that when I had little sleep, too much stress and no rest breaks that I spilled over with intensity when I had casual conversations. My emotions positive or negative were at a flashpoint. Again, I had to moderate my behavior. I was on the receiving end of this force one time when a parent was talking about advocating for their child. We were in an online chat. She happened to mention that she knew "her rights," she was going to go to court over a minor infraction in the classroom. I pointed out that they were her child's rights and lightly suggested that we as parents could perhaps to make an effort to build support with educators before we get litigious. The blow back of words was incredible. I was under the impression we were having a thoughtful chat. The barrage went on and on with no breaks for me to respond back. I was thinking, "Hey, why are you shooting your own? I'm on your side…we are on the same team!" I wanted to shut my laptop lid, but was strangely compelled or obligated to stay and read the response. I literally, physically shrunk back from my computer screen as the onslaught continued. As I reflected on this incident, I wondered in my own instance if I ever came to the table with an agenda ready pounce upon the very people who I was depending on to help me teach my child.

Team Building

Because autism is a communication/interaction disorder, it is vital to be united in the purpose of propelling a child with autism forward. Rules at school must be reinforced and upheld at home so that the continuity creates a less confusing atmosphere. By removing impediments to learning such as disorganization, sensory distractions, and unpredictability, the child is more focused on what is important.

At the appropriate time and in the appropriate setting, it is best to "spoon feed" information to people. With the previously mentioned intensity, we as parents tend to blurt or suddenly dump information for people to sort through. This especially happens with those parents who have not been able to get out of the house to socialize in frequent intervals. As a result of these encounters, people tend to form opinions and shy away from the energy we project. Parents can be misperceived as drama queens or individuals that thrive on having a crisis or need to create sense of drama in their lives. People apart from the family do not understand that the intensity that we experience at home can transfer to the relationships or demeanor outside the family unit. Now don't get me wrong, I know when I've looked a little wild eyed and had pent up energy that came from having frustration, lack of sleep or at least any type of respite.

I'm sure that I have come across in a strong manner, and tended to have verbal vomit, expelling far too much information than polite society allows.

Educators might get the impression that we like to complain about our children, when we only really wish to express, *and for them to appreciate*, the realness of our situation.

One of the best ways for educators to get a good grasp of what is going on in the home environment and get to know the child without listening to a litany of complaints or long involved stories, is by utilizing a journal. They can read the short notations in their spare time. My opinion is, the more information, the better. Not all at one time or in one large chunk, but the more details, the sharper in focus the picture of the child and the wider support can be given to student, educator, and parent.

Before the child attends any classroom, the groundwork has to be prepared and laid. If this is not done, the teacher not given the proper support and the foundation not stable for the classroom, the child will be destined to fail.

Now that the educator is apprised through journal notations of the challenges of trying to maintain a type of normalcy with a family impacted by an autistic individual, we as parents need to consider what steps to take towards organizing ourselves into effective team members.

Do your homework

Educate yourself about autism and your child's rights in the school system, *not just your child's rights!* You need to understand the "chain of command" in your school system. If you have a problem, you want to know where to start with the process of making changes and working together toward solutions before there is an issue. Meet and greet the teacher's boss, the school's district representative, the head of special education programs, even the superintendent himself, before any problems arise. Make an appointment, ask about their philosophy of the special programs in your district, shake their hand, show them your face. Introduce yourself and identify your child as well as their teacher. Don't do all of the talking but ask questions about their program listening to what they have to say, it may come in handy later. It is more difficult for schools to brush you off when they know you. When IEP time comes around, invite the teacher's boss to the IEP meetings (write them in as a team member), especially in the beginning. This is to ensure things go fairly, that telegraphs to the team members that you are familiar with their boss, and we all are ready to come to the table for the sake of educating your child.

Find out the philosophy of those who you will be working with, to locate support for your point of view. For example: when my daughter was in transition from elementary school to Jr. High, there was a huge turnover in the makeup of the IEP team. Many of them were unfamiliar with her history and therefore were making decisions based on limited knowledge. Most of them wanted to take her off of an IEP, put her into a behavioral program (she never had behavioral issues) and take her from the educational model of total inclusionism in the classroom only to place her into a pre-made program in their self contained classroom. This would not have suited her needs, but would have been cost efficient for the school. When I informed the rest of the team that their plan would be totally out of the question, I had key people to lend me their support. The professionals who I spent time building a rapport of mutual respect and vision over the years were there when I needed them.

Develop a "team" mindset.

There are questions that I would ask myself. Through all of the goals in the process, I would ask myself the same questions: "Where is Kim now? Where do I want her to be? How do I get her there?" By utilizing the responses to those questions, I was able to generate some ideas for plans of action. I wrote them down and came to the IEP meetings ready to address many of the unreached goals and submitted some of my own suggestions. Why should the educators have all of the influence over what goals should be focused upon, after all it had to be supported at home which affected my time and effort. I wanted and needed to be part of the process. In order to be prepared to take my place at the education planning table, I jotted down some thoughts on paper:

Define for yourself what role you will have as a team member.
- Are you going to be an advocate for your child?
- What do you want for your child?
- Are you willing to put forth ideas and strategies to contribute your child's education program?
- Are you going to be an active or passive member of the team?
- Do you want to rubberstamp any IEP that the professionals develop or are you going to get involved in the process?

Assess your strengths and weaknesses.

Are you outspoken? Then discuss your ideas with a refreshing frankness. Do you write well? Write the superintendent about how well your education program is going. Do you have ideas about how the process can be made easier? Talk to the principal. If you are good at socializing, networking, or coordination, think of how you might utilize that attribute to its fullest potential. Perhaps you are a creative problem solver and you think "outside the box", try thinking about what special needs your child has, and how you can use your strengths to your child's advantage.

I was a parent sapped of energy, feeling helpless to change my situation. I hated to waste time, it made me feel unproductive. As the need to supervise Kim at night grew I had to stay up with her, I used the time to bake. It helped me stay awake as well as giving an outlet for my sorely tested nerves. I felt productive and focused which in itself was quite a feat. Since our family couldn't eat it all themselves and I wanted to show the Early Intervention staff how much I appreciated them, I gave the EI program many types of baked goods. I continued my baking on into the years we spent in the public school system. It was just a little thing, but the teachers felt appreciated. I wrote little notes to the teachers. At first, when I would drop by the classroom, the teachers appeared to be tense and on their guard. After I popped in with treats and little notes of appreciation, I noticed they relaxed when I came into the room. In other words my presence was not the cause for alarm, I wasn't there to criticize them, just a friendly word then I was gone.

At the place where my husband worked, they gave out "Good Job" certificates. If a person called up to say how well he performed his job, he received acknowledgement, a pat on the back. Having started my education towards becoming a teacher in college, I was well aware of how motivating positive reinforcement can be. I applied this when it came to the teachers and staff at school. I began to send notes with positive messages telling them that I appreciated their extra efforts, and acknowledged how challenging it was to have my daughter with special needs in the typical classroom. Acknowledgment means so much. I wasn't necessarily emphasizing their skills as good teachers but rather supporting and investing in the teachers that they *could* become. They didn't disappoint, although they had no training as special education teachers, they grew into the abilities they needed to teach my child side by side with her typical peers.

Whatever your weaknesses are, if you can think of any, try to down play them. If meetings are not your strong suits, because I know they are not mine, keep them brief, focused and to the point. I can be almost diplomatic to a fault. I wanted to be more firm as an advocate for my child, it was almost painful to stand up and say that I disagreed with a strategy or program. This was always an issue. Because of this, I had to work harder behind the scenes to convince professionals of my vision of inclusion. I found that confrontation was not my strong suit, but building support was, so I concentrated on doing just that.

I had to keep my energy in check. I had a shorter fuse for the fact that I was so sleep deprived, my attention span being continually divided. At the same time, it was difficult to concentrate in meetings, my brain wanted to shut down to a sleeping mode because I wasn't physically engaged. More than once I had to ask for clarification or for someone to repeat themselves. Know your limits and don't stretch yourself too thin by over extending your resources. Plan to contribute in a small way and if it works well, build on it. Teachers welcome all kinds of help. There are so many things that can be done to support teachers. Find your niche. If you can't find one, make one!!

Develop a communication system between home and school.

It doesn't matter whether it is email, journal, notes or telephone calls. In order to coordinate and maintain the level of services in all areas, school, church, respite. Communication is a MUST! Where ever Kim went, the journal followed her. It didn't take a trained individual to figure out that if Kim had a significant reaction to the setting around her, that it should be noted and of course. If she was injured or something unusual occurred, it all had to be logged into the notebook. Respite Care providers, grandparents, substitute teachers as well as others wrote their observations and impressions while Kim was in their care. Since a functionally nonverbal autistic child is unable to come home for school or other event and tell you about their day, good or bad, it's the next best thing to being there. I cannot convey enough about how vital it is that everyone is united in purpose. Autism creates fractions, the way to remedy this is to assemble the parts to make a whole.

Now that you've done all of this preparation to make yourself into a fantastic team member, it's time to put it into practice.

Call meetings– to make sure that the education staff is "on the same page" with your vision of your child's Individual Education Program (IEP). Keep up to date with goals, children develop at different rates during the year. Children often reach goals weeks or months after the initial goals are written. Sometimes if a strategy comes to mind on how to boost your child over a learning hurdle, you want all of the team to have a chance to give their input. When Kim began meeting IEP objectives, we had to scramble to keep up.

Prepare professionals– with personal information helpful to the staff to get to know your child. This can be done by writing a one page note or videotaping your child in a setting that is not stressful. Professionals often do not have time to go observe the child. You know your child's quirks, behaviors, fears, sensitivities. Who better than you to give the important information needed to ensure your child gets a wonderful start? My daughter always sounded worse on paper than she looked in real life. After teachers met her, they began to relax a bit. She was still a challenge, but the image they had in their head was far more intimidating than any problem that arose.

Plugged in– Make sure all of the team is "Plugged In." Problems can arise when some team members are absent. Let's face it, they have doctor's appointments, families, and things going on in their private lives too. However, if they miss important information, this may cause a problem later when there is decision making. If team member miss meetings, keep them up to date by placing a quick telephone call or jot a note, especially if you need to give them your opinion about a particular issue addressed in the meeting. Be punctual for meetings just as though you would be for a job. You will not impress anyone by being habitually late. Make sure that if you cannot make a meeting to give plenty of advanced notice so that educators can make other plans and choose an alternate date for postponement.

Inform– the group about your willingness as a member to participate as part of the team. Describe to them what you are doing at home or at school to contribute. Educators are not at home with you. They have no idea how much the structure that you have implemented or all that you have invested in time, energy and effort, in maintaining goals at home. Ask them to share with you about lessons in the classroom and target those skills at home as well. Teachers were surprised that when Kim was learning a certain concept in school, the lesson was supported and repeated in the home environment.

I have found that many educators take a cue for how vigorously the parents want to pursue educational goals by how much the parent wants to be involved in the process. So many times I have witnessed educators who have come up with a healthy robust IEP, only to not have it supported and it falls flat. There is nothing that takes the wind out of the sails of a teacher, autism specialist or assistant, like coming up with an exciting strategy and only being able to work with the child during school hours.

You must understand as a parent, you set the tone for how robustly the educational goals should be pursued. It is a parent driven. You cannot afford to be a passive participant, physically sitting at the table but not mentally and emotionally involved in the process. Not only does your child need you to be their advocate and their voice, but also their representative to ensure the proper amount of services. Most professionals are reluctant to implement aggressive programs for children unless the family is "onboard" too. An IEP should put forth goals regarding the child in a way that a family can support it.

Plan for Success/Prepare for Failure!

Professionals and parents always make wonderful detailed plans that we hope will be implemented with success. During the planning session for Kim's IEP, we had written well thought out goals, strategies and scheduling systems. I really shook things up when I put my pencil down and said, "What are we going to do if there is a problem? Let's say that Kim has a total meltdown, she is flailing out of control and some children might get hurt." The teachers exchanged looks. Immediately, the teacher said that she would announce to the class to join hands, and file out to an unscheduled recess. The assistant piped up with the fact that she would be the one to stay with my daughter. If in the case that Kim didn't calm down after the class had been cleared, she offered to call help from the special programs room. There was someone from that room appointed to become familiar with Kim so that it would not be a strange presence coming into her vicinity. We worked on the idea with specific details. No one would touch my child, approach her or overwhelm her in anyway. They had never once considered or suggested phoning the police. *In this day and age when police are being called to handle an issue of an autistic child in schools, something is drastically WRONG!* Law enforcement should be called only if "the child is going to hurt themselves or others." To me, this issue highlights the need to build support with the parent and reveals the lack of training and skills on the educator's part as well as the lack of planning in the IEP process.

Just so that everyone was all in agreement on the team and to ensure the safety of the other students as well as the child with autism, plan for worst case scenario. Write down on paper what measures the staff will take, what the students will be instructed to do. This way the teacher is confident having a plan into place where no one will get hurt and if there are concerns from other parents, the teacher can reassure them that there is a contingency plan at the ready. Communication is an absolute must!

Volunteer– for a FEW field trips especially in the beginning when they are just getting to know your child. That way you can head off any crisis situations before they arise and also give educators time to get to see your child in a new environment. Teachers and staff will appreciate your willingness to help.

Give feedback– not necessarily criticism. Otherwise, how is a teacher to know what works and what does not. Choose a time and place that is not rushed such as the transition between class times. Bring some cookies or something to munch on as you talk or share a cup of coffee or Chai tea together. Don't go to a huge expense or trouble. A former professor of a college I attended, taught his students: KISMIF- Keep It Simple/Make It Fun! If you don't have time to stop by or the teacher is extremely busy, send notes or expression of appreciation. When something works well, *reinforce it!*

- First and foremost be your child's advocate.
- Write into the IEP when and if you want your child's disability disclosed.
- Build in strategies– Plan for Success/Prepare of Failure.

Professionals and parents always make wonderful detailed plans that we hope will be implemented with success. But what if something goes totally awry?

Acknowledge Each Other's Challenges
Many professionals overloaded with the idea of one child having so many educational goals, may be quick to point out that there is more than just one child with educational needs in the classroom.

Professionals also need to be aware that there is probably more than one specialist in contact with this family during the course of a week or month. There can be Respite Care providers, Equestrian Therapy experts, Speech Therapists, Occupational Therapists, not to mention medical personnel, among many others. It can be a tricky job being a parent, trying to coordinate the services that a disabled child requires and to maintain continuity throughout. Parents need to prioritize goals in order to convey which objectives are most immediate. Focusing on present strategies and looking to the near future at emerging skills is a good way to keep within the scope of the IEP.

As you know, parents have a heavy load. At times, family and friends don't know what to say or do, so they say and do nothing for fear of doing the wrong thing. Unless a parent has an extraordinary family relationship, support is rare. Many parents feel isolated, abnormal, and out of step with typical families.

Educators are doing so much more than just teaching. Nowadays they are expected to council the child, watch over them for signs of abuse, and teach them many things that used to be taught in the home. Their roles have expanded to the point that they are stretched very thin. Often times, in the field of education, the lack of funding means that they will be adding more children to an already crowded classroom.

Giving each other a word of encouragement is one of the best ways that I know strengthen support. It is not easy to be an educator or a parent, but we do our best and need the acknowledgement of our efforts and our struggles. It is incredible what a kind word can do to restore hope, it is like a breath of fresh air when everything around us can feel oppressive and negative. There were many days that I lived on the words of kindness that people shared with me.

Offer yourself as a resource

Whether you are a parent or an education professional, offer yourself. As a parent, you have insight to how your child functions. You may have answers to why a strategy will or won't work with your child and have the most observation time of anyone else. You must recognize that you possess an incredible wealth of experience regarding your loved one with autism.

Professionals have many resources at their disposal to utilize in the team process. They have knowledge as to teaching methods. They have the ability to access services that enhance your child's learning abilities.

By respecting each other's position and making the most of the assets that are sitting around the IEP team table, work together, to find the best aspects of your relationship and bring them out! Toss some ideas around with the parent and the rest of the team, make everyone part of the process.

Avoid Pitfalls

As a professional, you have the knowledge, you are proficient at what you do, you receive monetary compensation as well as garner respect for your expertise and on top of all of that, you have compassion. There are pitfalls that professionals commonly make when communicating with parents of autistic children.

Trying to relate with a typical example

Autism differs from physically impairments and this is where many people unfamiliar with the disability falls short of being able to relate. For instance, when I went to pick up my daughter from a week long camp, I found she was off in another building packing her things. I struck up a conversation with the camp nurse. She was telling me of this boy who had lost a leg in some sort of accident, "but it didn't seem to slow him down at all." "He is able to do everything that everyone else does…" She went on to highlight all of the instances of how this missing limb actually posed no barrier to this individual. There was nothing this boy couldn't do and he made jokes about it.

Then she switched the conversation to Kim and how well she had done at camp. I was beginning to get the idea that her point was that I was the one who had an emotional attachment to my daughter's disability, that I needed some sort of gratification that Kim was indeed special. That I was much more into this "disability thing" than what my daughter actually displayed. Little was she aware of the years of preparation of scheduling, and desensitization so that Kim could attend camp. Kim was so terrified of the setting years before, that she screamed, threw a tantrum and insisted that we dump her older sister Marcia off without so much as a tour of the camp or a kiss goodbye.

This nurse is not the only one that I have come across that has these views. People dear to me, whose child didn't have a disability that permeated every thought and consideration of their day, often would say, "I just treat my child with a disability just like all of my other children." This was often a dagger in my heart because I would have *preferred* to be able to treat Kim like everyone else, but when I don't make allowances or accommodations for her disability, that puts her at a disadvantage.

A professional may not realize it when it comes out of their mouths. It is such a natural thing to try to comfort someone by saying "oh, that's normal" or "I've done that myself!" In some way, we are thinking that we are mitigating the sting of a humiliating event or assuring another person that it is such a common place occurrence that it has also happened to them.

When I brought up the fact that my daughter who was in seventh grade was not using the telephone, a teacher said that it was ok. "…besides, teenage conversations are really meaningless anyway. They don't impart important information. It's full of teenage drama and gossip". Then this teacher went so far as to model just how trivial a typical teenage conversation would be by pantomiming a phone to her ear.

As I sat there, she had no idea how much it would hurt me from my perspective. I would give anything for someone to just call my daughter up, even if it was a conversation over nothing. I would have been thrilled if my daughter was able to say something spontaneous in answer to a question, instead of the echolalia that she in which she was trapped. The teacher had missed the whole point of teenagers connecting, not necessarily communicating, but bonding through common experience.

When I bring up these issues to address during meetings, the purpose is not to complain or to evoke sympathy for my situation. It is to bring up a valid concern that I have in order to address strategies and goal writing. I do not expect professionals to relate to the experience in any way unless they indeed have come across this particular circumstance involving autism or disability much like it.

"Me too!" Syndrome

I was at her IEP bringing up the social skills that were just not developing. Autism as a certain deficit of skills in particular areas, it is very distinctive. Every concern I brought up, this one teacher would say, "Oh, my son does that too". She continued on for several more points were on the table for discussion.

After awhile, I felt like stopping the meeting and asking her if she ever thought of looking into getting her son diagnosed.

I wanted to know what he perserverated on and how long did it last? Hours? Days? Weeks? Did he keep her up all hours of the night perching on or galloping off the furniture because his body could not relax and go to sleep? Did he pull out his hair and stim at the light? Did he relate to objects rather than people?

I wanted to tell her that it took a long, precise and personally excruciating process for my daughter to be tested and found autistic. Many professionals have taken painstaking care over many years to ensure this diagnosis is indeed correct. The teacher wanted to "normalize" my experience by stating she had a similar experience with her own child. What she had intended to do was to try and relate to my experience using her child as an example and therefore take the significance out of what I had experienced. She had no idea or *respect* for where this journey of autism had taken me. Believe me when I say, given the chance, with only a few sentences, I can wipe the most all knowing smile and patronizing look off of anyone's face. Please try to avoid the "me too" pitfall.

Not the Only Child

An IEP would not be complete without an educator reminding me that my daughter was not the only child in the classroom or that there was another child ("Little Johnny") who had more issues that did not receive near the services as my child.

First of all, I should not have to be apprised of how many children who have special needs are also in my daughter's classroom. That is a staffing issue. During the IEP process I was careful to ask reasonable accommodations for my daughter's needs, no more and no less. It is up to the educators to figure out how best to deliver the services needed. Little Johnny's mother needs to bring up his issues at their own IEP meeting. It is not my concern to evaluate any child other than my own and to do so would be illegal. Please keep in mind the singular child while discussing the IEP.

Creating Communication/How much parent involvement

Much depends on where the parent is in the acceptance or denial of the disability. Some parents reject the label of autism altogether. Many parents appear to be obsessed with information of autism, while others would rather try homeopathic means to cure their child. By asking the simple question of how much they want to be involved in the education program, you can ascertain whether or not they would be open to keeping education goals consistent on both levels (home and school) Creating a partnership with a parent to support lessons from the classroom not only helps the child learn, but also gives a strength and consistency.

Give Parents Room to Grow

I bought a coffee cup a few years ago that said, "This is not the life I ordered". Remember parents of disabled children are not born, we are made. Having a child with autism dramatically changed my life immediately after she was born. Upon her diagnoses 3 years later, I had to come to grips with the fact that I could not change my life back to the way it was and had to find a way to cope with a new kind of future. I was a little resentful that this was not the path that I had chosen. I was never the type of person who was in the front, policy making, mover and shaker. Somehow, I had to find a way to step out of my former self who was a behind the scenes person and become more influential in my daughter's education process.

I have been so fortunate to have professionals who mentored me, took me under their wing to teach me what I needed to do for my child. Since there were so many different teaching styles and personalities, so many different points of view that I was exposed to, that I have a wonderful palette of experiences to draw from. They helped shape me into a more effective, better educated advocate for my child. Give parents room to grow into their role as a team member and advocate.

Oh, and by the way, I wouldn't trade my way of life now for any other.

We are all in this together

We are continually trying to find answers/therapies to help our child and can be easily overwhelmed by a complicated and sometimes volatile daily life.

We are all in this together, meaning that the main objective is to work toward the common goal, focused on the very special, individual needs of a child with autism. Professionals and parents alike want to support the child towards success. We can't accomplish this all alone, by understanding each other's challenges, exchanging ideas for strategies, and at times encouraging one another, we are creating a strong team. That can't help but have a positive impact on a child, any child.

CHAPTER 7

Building Support Between Physicians and Parents

Building Support Between Physicians and Others

This chapter is very important to me because I believe if there would have been better communication between the doctor and I, Kim's autism could have been identified much sooner than 3 years of age.

For the first two years of her life, I took Marcia to the same physician for "well child" visits. He performed all of the standard developmental tests. Marcia was an amiable child. When the doctor went to examine Kim, she wailed so much, and was so upset, that no one could be heard. She was frightened by the hygienic paper on the examination table. The sound of it crinkling and rustling with each movement exacerbated the situation. As the doctor tried to speak over the screaming infant, I in turn, couldn't hear him. Finally he gave up and said that Kim was very healthy. As we made subsequent visits, they often ended the same way with me leaving without having asked or answered questions.

After a few months, when we came to visit, there were some noticeable changes. Kim of course was older, larger to wrangle and just as upset. My appearance was drastically altered. I was wearing my husband's flannel shirts, sometimes his jeans. My hair was not fashioned into any style just I had mentioned in earlier chapters. The doctor assumed that my family had fallen on hard financial times so he urged me to take Kim to a free clinic for vaccinations rather than his office. At this point I was hoping that he would find whatever was going on with my youngest daughter, but because she was so healthy, there was really no reason to take her to him other than getting her shots. Even though he urged me to go elsewhere for vaccinations, I stubbornly went for two more appointments until he took me aside and explained I should take her to the county clinic.

Perhaps if I had been able to tell the doctor, impress upon him the devastating effect of having a child who didn't require sleep, who rarely had a break from screeching, who was upset in every environment, Kim and I could have gotten help sooner.

To solve this problem, I would like to propose that physicians examining infants and young children have a nurse or assistant take the child out of the room so that parent and physician can speak uninterrupted. Had I been able to think clearly, I should have taken time to sit down and write out my questions on a piece of paper so that I could communicate my concerns and submit it to be placed into Kim's chart the day before our scheduled appointment. Since he was our family physician, I would think that the change in my demeanor and clothing might have given him a clue to our struggle at home. Again, I would advise to go by the rule, if Momma/Papa don't look happy/healthy, it might be an indicator that something is going wrong in the family atmosphere.

We are so fortunate in this day and age of autism. When Kim was a toddler, most physicians expected to see very few cases in their career, if at all. Nowadays the numbers juggle between 1 in every 150 children or lower.

Because autism is not necessarily physically apparent, with no definitive medical tests to confirm that it exists in your child, family, friends, teachers and even physicians may be dubious about diagnosis

Fifteen years ago, one mother contacted me about her son. He was diagnosed by an Early Intervention autism specialist. In order for her to get Social Security assistance for her child, he had to be seen by a government appointed psychiatrist. Upon seeing the child, the professional proclaimed him "normal." She was in tears as she told me that she had bought so easily into the idea that he was autistic. I went over the stereotypical behaviors and deficits of autism with her over the phone. Although I'm not a licensed professional, based on my experience, her answers told me that the diagnosis was correct. She scheduled another appointment with the psychiatrist to test again; he came up with his same conclusion. Vacillating between whether he was autistic or not was more than what she could deal with at the time.

Imagine how hard it is for those closest to you to accept that throwing tantrums of frustration, having inappropriate social behavior, besides other issues, is a disability rather than an ill behaved child. Especially, when a well trained professional cannot recognize it!

Thanks to autism awareness and more sensitive diagnostic testing, autism is recognized and intervention recommended. It is imperative that we as parents be well prepared for a physician. First of all, we must do our research. Ask around in your circle of friends who have children with special needs. Look for someone who will listen to your concerns and not dismiss you out of hand. After choosing an appropriate physician (you may have to go through a few to find the right one) then make an appointment to talk to them about your child. Bring short notes regarding your child to be put into the file.

Things that should be in the file:
- Whether or not your child is verbal
- Odd reactions to painful stimuli
- Level of development
- Things that you think he/she should know that are pertinent to his treating your child so that they can get the best examination possible.

All of this preparation work will pay off when you take your child to see the physician for the first time. For example; Kim does *not* like to be touched under the chin. The doctor respecting that issue, does not touch her but instructs her to turn her head so he can examine her. He tells her where and when he is going to touch her during an examination. By keeping her informed of his movements and the area he is viewing, she doesn't tense up, is not afraid and has respect for the doctor. Whenever an examination is coming up and there is a health concern, I write down my current observations by utilizing the journal and drop it by the office one to 2 days before the appointment so that the doctor can become familiar with what questions he needs to ask of the patient or parent.

Now that Kim is an adult, he asks her questions. Often times she doesn't know the answer right away, and we can't take up the physician's time by having her sit to think of a response. By giving the doctor a clue as to what he is looking for, helps to narrow down the field of questions he asks, which makes his job easier and streamlined. Physicians have only minutes to make observations and diagnosis. Hopefully by combing over the material in the journal, you can narrow down the symptoms of your child's sickness to whether it is mental or physical. You are the constant observer of your child's behavior and physical well being. As a parent, you are a vital participant in this process.

Physician's side of working with parents

More than once in my life I have had to wait for long periods of time in the pediatrician's waiting room while Kim practically climbed the walls. At first, she was distressed because it was a strange place upon arrival. She was in high stress mode and not interested in playing with toys or reading a book. As the time between our wait and the actual seeing the doctor increased because of unforeseen delays, Kim was pushed past her "goodness" or "goodwill factor." She only had so much manageable time to be able to function somewhat appropriately in a room until there was total meltdown into throwing a tantrum. At this time, usually an examining room would open up and we were escorted into the hallway. Once in the very small room, I went into high alert mode for the fact that the room was packed with expensive equipment. There were drawers that Kim wanted to pull out and dump, electrical cords, and interesting looking tools. The doctor arrived much later after I wrestled with my daughter, trying to anticipate her next move and head her off before she could do any damage. She was whipped into a frenzy with all of these strange objects and her mother not allowing her to touch. At this point, her pulse would be taken and found that her heart was beating so wildly, that an accurate rate could not be taken. When the doctor wanted to speak to me regarding her health, I could not devote my full attention because again, I was keeping Kim out of the medical paraphernalia and she was screeching at the top of her lungs.

I will not pretend to tell physicians how to run their offices. However, there are some tips that may be helpful when treating a patient with autism.

- Many autistic people do not have a reference for time so they do not know when the examination will begin or end, which can cause anxiety.
- Reducing the time of waiting in offices packed with equipment will help the parent be able to participate in giving helpful information.
- Have one of your assistants take the child for a moment so that the parent can hear and take in important information about medical treatment.

Physicians need to recognize that your child is not a statistic and treat the autistic person as an individual. We ran into problems when a doctor read about the tendencies for autistic girls towards a certain serious condition. The physician made radical changes to Kim's diet and her whole way of life based on what was written in studies about girls having autism. The doctor had not taken a family history, or asked any questions about Kim's current diet. The result was disastrous.

CHAPTER 8

Building Support Between Law Enforcement and Others

Building Support Between Law Enforcement and Others
In the United States

This will probably be the most controversial chapter because of the nature of law enforcement. Just about everyone, by the time that they have become parents, have interacted with a police officer, whether receiving a traffic violation ticket or an emergency situation. In either case, many times the experience is one involving high stress and in hindsight is interpreted as being a negative ordeal. Parents and police officers, are the two groups that I am most passionate about and I must address this issue so that hopefully it can effect change, open dialogue, to create safety between each other.

Early encounters with law enforcement officials often influence how we feel toward safety authorities, often times these emotions are transferred to our children. There are even a handful of parents who inadvertently build fear into their children by threatening to "call the police" and "they will take you to jail," if their child does not comply with what they are requesting. They use the officer as an aversive to motivate but do not realize they are instilling anxiety. Sometimes children gather their impressions off of the television. Nowadays TV shows and commercials can be violent, loud and frightening. How many times do we go a little faster on the freeway without realizing how fast we are going and when we spot a police car feel alarm? I'm raising my hand! Whatever your opinion on authority figures, parents need to ensure that they have built a proper foundation so that whether their children are small or adult, when encountering safety officials they will be safe.

Children, even autistic ones may not have the ability to verbally interpret the concepts of what they are absorbing but, the impression that they gather may be the wrong one. The problem usually doesn't present itself until the child grows up and as a teenager has an encounter with a police officer. First of all, there is a heightened sense of awareness, secondly, it is unexpected, which usually derails our typical thought processes. For the average teen, it is not much of an inconvenience but to the autistic individual it can be dangerous. When an officer stops a suspicious acting individual, a person who is in an area that looks like they don't belong, they will stop to talk to that person. Now everyone has the right to walk or be anywhere they wish to go, that is not in dispute, however many crimes are solved in this way. A friendly inquiry doesn't hurt anyone except sometimes when there is a miscommunication. The problem occurs when both sides do not understand the motivation of the other. This is where I hope to build the bridge.

When a police officer approaches any individual to ask questions, they "read" the person's body language. Does the person look nervous? Do they look shifty (furtive eye contact) and (no eye contact) evasive? Do they avoid answering questions in a forthright manner? Imagine what it would be like for an autistic person to be approached by a stranger in a uniform who asks questions. First of all, the person with autism may feel a panic or at least be uncomfortable, as though they did something wrong. Then the police officer's gaze is intent on gathering information, perhaps making the autistic person not want to look in the direction of their face, and therefore appearing to have something to hide. All of the questions are auditory which often plays to a weaker side of autism, making it difficult to process information in real time. Then it takes time to formulate a response and perhaps because of nervousness, the ability to use spontaneous language for answers may not be present. Meanwhile, the information that the officer is gathering is: A profile of a person who looks like they don't belong in the area, who is looking uncomfortable and appears to be reluctant to give information. The officer find this developing profile as something that he needs to find more facts, so he inquires deeper. The longer the officer questions, the more suspicious this person becomes. The body language coupled with the communication deficit all telegraphs the wrong information to the officer and unfortunately, the newspaper is riddled with stories of scenarios just like this with an escalation and someone getting hurt. What the officer doesn't realize is that he is looking at a person who has a hidden disability.

How then can we circumvent this situation from happening between anyone, let alone autistic individuals? The best way to prevent problems is with education split into three elements: Law Enforcement, Parent, and Child.

The Parent Component

Parents are such a vital component to the education process and can do this quite simply by taking opportunities to teach the child by giving facts about motivations of the police officer. Even though officers do many visits to school classrooms to make positive impressions, it is up to you to take the panic and anxiety out of the unknown and practice with your children whenever you see a police person.

Here is a list for small children:

- There are laws to keep all people safe.
- A police officer could also be known as a safety officer.
- The officer is human. He has a family; he is just like you and me. Being a police officer is his job.
- The officer is there to make sure all people follow rules and keep people from hurting themselves or others.
- Sometimes an officer needs to stop people from doing things that can be dangerous to themselves or others.
- If you are lost, hurt or you need help, find a police officer.

Hopefully as the child grows older, they will understand what role the police officer plays in society. I believe it is the parent's job to prepare autistic children for life experiences. By doing so, we take the mystery and much of the anxiety out of a situation that could possibly spiral out of control.

A list for an older child or teenager:

- Officers often need information to find out if a crime has been committed. He does this by stopping people to ask questions.
- If you are stopped to be asked questions, answer the best that you can. First offer your ID. Card. If you don't know the answers to the questions, it is alright. Tell the officer that you don't know.
- Tell the police officer "I am doing the best that I can." So that he will understand that you are trying to comply.
- When or if an officer puts you in to the back of his car- it does not always mean that you are under arrest. It is for your safety and the safety of others until the officer finds out all of the facts.
- Never run from a police officer. They will chase you! They will try to stop you. The best thing to do is stop and obey the commands of the officer. Remember there is always time to explain your side of the story.
- If the officer puts handcuffs on your wrists, this does not necessarily mean that you are under arrest. This is a way to keep you both safe until he can find out the information he needs to know. If the hand-

cuffs are uncomfortable, if you ask nicely, the officer is more inclined to adjust them. Courtesy and politeness goes a long way when you need help.

- If a police officer takes you to the police station, this does not mean you are under arrest. Sometimes it is the best way to have time to talk calmly with police officers and they can call your parents or someone you know.

I am enclosing a sample of a card should accompany identification so that any officer of the law can get the information that they need:

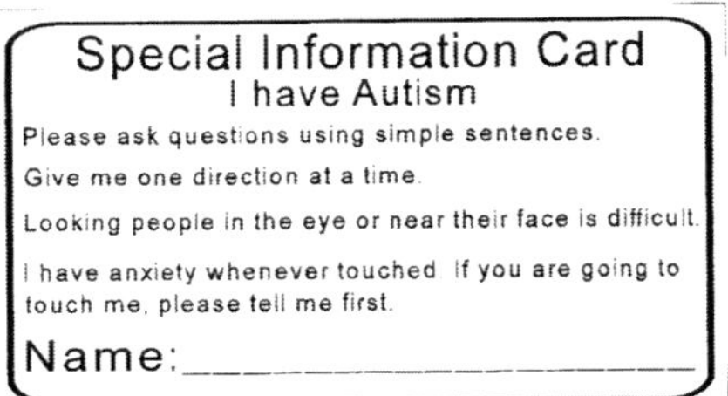

Parents should practice the submitting the card by role playing. Switch roles and let your teenager be the officer. This will help them identify with the person of authority. This is a way to desensitize your child to the situation and therefore gives them a script to work off of if the case ever arrives. Preparation is key for any person having autism. By doing so, it removes the fear of the unknown, thereby reducing anxiety and creating a situation where everybody will be more likely to be successful in a simple encounter.

Now you can argue the finer points of the problems with the established police force and the wrongs that have been done. I want to focus on safety for everyone, police officer and autistic/disabled individual. What is important is that everyone comes home unharmed at the end of the day. The rest can sort itself out later.

Law Enforcement in the United States

Coming from a family police officers and having been a part of the extensive "family" of law enforcement officers. I've had the occasion to engage them in conversation from time to time and of course disability happened to enter the discussion. On one particular....an officer told me of a brief encounter in passing with another police officer. Somehow the subject of individuals with "special needs" cropped up. The fellow officer had mentioned that he/she could "tell a person was disabled just by looking at them." Even though my friend had pointed out that there are many hidden disabilities, the fellow officer held to the opinion that they could detect a disability by sight. Of course I was shocked by this but this story just highlighted the fact that we have a long way to go in some areas to build support and respect for individuals with special needs. I realize that this is not the case for all departments, but even if one person out of each department shared this opinion, then it could put the rest of the officers at risk.

The way to build support in this instance would be to volunteer to give a workshop to educate officers regarding communication/interaction disorders which are not apparent, even to the most trained professional. Make the police department aware that if they encounter a suspicious person who isn't able to give good eye contact, unable to offer appropriate information, that they must not assume that a person is shifty or has something to hide. The issue may not be non compliance but a disability. When they are looking for identification in the wallet, there also may be an information card that could provide further information and help answer some of the questions that they have about this individual. Once locating such a card they should be aware that the individual may need an advocate to speak for them or give appropriate answers to their questions. The card also explains that the person may have an adverse reaction to being touched. Having the person wait in the police car may give the person a sense of safety until the advocate arrives. Taking a little extra time to find out the facts adds to the safety of both officer and individual.

- Officers would be taught to look for Special Information Card when viewing individual's ID.
- Officers would learn that not every disability is physically apparent ie: unusual gait or facial features or expression.
- "Suspicious behavior" may be the result of the inability to give eye contact, mental stress because of the "surprise" of being stopped, the urge to flee because of the inability to verbally explain what they are doing and the inability in "real time" to process the information from the questions being asked.
- Stuttering or stammering is not an indication of guilt or manufactured lie.
- Anxiety and sense of panic can escalate in conjunction with the length of the interview.
- As a result of heightened anxiety, touching a person exhibiting symptoms may cause them to strike back or bolt, not as a result of hostility but from fear and possibly because of painful tactile stimulation.

Making assumptions based on body language is probably the worst thing that can happen for an individual with autism. When under duress which can be caused by any out of the ordinary event, such as being stopped which heightens anxiety. Unless a person was familiar with autism or have been educated regarding the condition, most likely the subtle tell-tale symptoms would confuse or elude even the most well trained officer.

What a police officer should do:

When an officer finds that the person he has stopped has an interaction/communication disorder and exhibiting signs of stress an officer should:

- Speak simply. Complicated sentences are hard to process when a person is nervous.
- When giving directions, give one direction at a time. Do not give two and three step directions! Give time for the person to comply between directives.
- Be specific. Say exactly what you mean.
- Sometimes by using a monotone voice a person with autism finds it easier to understand because inflexion can be distracting to what is being said.
- Step back slightly, just by giving that extra personal space, an autistic person can regain some composure.
- Be reassuring that everything is ok.
- Do not touch. If you *have* to touch, tell them where you are going to touch the person eg. *"I'm going to touch you lightly on the shoulder to move you here."*

Police officers are often the primary contact when emergencies happen. Knowing who you are dealing with and being educated about the special needs population only makes you a better officer.

By addressing the part of the parent to build a positive image of a police officer being a person whose only interest is in keeping citizens of the community safe, we can begin to take the fear out of being encountered by a law enforcement officer. If parents lay the groundwork of practicing with their teenage children about giving their Special Information card, many needless misunderstandings can be averted. With law enforcement being trained about appropriately stopping a person with a communication/interaction disorder, misunderstandings can be averted and everyone goes home safely at the end of the day.

Creating this balance of information and forming a deliberate connection to this environment was the cornerstone of our "Prepare for success; plan for failure" philosophy. By preparing our children with their encounters with professional such as teachers, law enforcement and physicians, we can more easily receive the services we require for daily living.

Conclusion

Birthday Celebration

Before Kim's formal diagnosis of autism at the age of three, I had phoned her EI preschool teacher Mary, and asked if we should just skip the observance of her birthday. I explained how, in the past, she had screeched, frantic and frustrated. Afraid of everything and everyone, she was miserable at these "celebrations." I told her that Kim didn't like anything we bought her, and she liked the look of wrapped presents, but she threw tantrums when anyone tried to reveal the contents inside, as though opening the gift were somehow breaking it.

Mary said we didn't need to skip the observance. She instructed me to find pictures of all the elements of a birthday party and go over the steps of it with Kim. I thought sarcastically, "Oh yeah, right. If we just show her, everything will be all right." However, I didn't let my voice betray my thoughts, and I asked about presents.

Mary thought for a moment and said, "Well, you know she likes bubbles."

"Bubbles?" I said, "That isn't much of a gift."

"She really likes them, and isn't that what's important?" Mary spoke kindly.

"Okay," I said, but I still thought, "But a fifty-cent jar of bubbles isn't much of a gift."

I combed through all the photographs we had, loose in a box, and came up with birthday pictures from the year before. We didn't have many pictures of Kim because I refused to take them when she was unhappy, and that, unfortunately, was most of the time. I gathered those I did have, and placing her on my lap (which she immediately wanted to vacate) I half-heartedly went through the motions of familiarizing her with the birthday party ritual. There were pictures of the cake, of Kim, of her grandparents, and of presents. I went over the pictures with her three times and then brought out a candle, lit it, and blew it out.

I had her practice blowing out the candle while Marcia and I sang the birthday song at barely over a whisper, so as not to over-stimulate her. Hours later, as the grandparents arrived, I instructed them to come in quietly and not to wish her a pleasant special day in excited tones. They filed in, silently, as if this were a mournful occasion rather than the joyous one that it should be. I informed them of the order of events according to how I explained it to Kim.

"This is ridiculous." I said to myself. "Parties should be spontaneous—enthusiastic." Because everyone was familiar with Kim's behavior at these times, they were braced for anything, but all was quiet. Silently and without ceremony, we introduced the gifts, sans paper, and everyone held their breaths to see what Kim might do.

She appropriately asked by signing for help to get the bubble jar opened. Miraculously, Kim didn't throw the very plain-faced, six-inch doll with the small feeding bottle my mom had brought, but when she began to use the bottle appropriately, Mom enthusiastically said, "Good girl!" Immediately, Kim postured her hands and screeched. When no one moved or made a fuss, she calmed down and began to focus again. We looked at one another. It was working!

We moved on to the cake. Holding Kim's fingers back from plunging into the cake and, more important, from the burning candles, we sang "Happy Birthday" in low tones, not wanting to burst the bubble of this incredible moment. We all could sense that something great was happening here, and we were willing to do what we could to prolong it. My father gave me a kiss just before leaving. With tears in his eyes, his voice cracking, he said, "She was almost normal tonight."

As I have said before, I have done just about anything for a word of hope. The hope being that the situation that had spun out of control could change. Before any type of transformation, before any alteration of the path our family was on, I had to become a believer. I had to believe something could turn around the trend of hopelessness which was compounded by the condition of depression, brought on by the lack of support from friends and family as well as not having the education or training to deal with an undiagnosed autistic individual. Change cannot occur by just wistfully wishing that life would be different, and accepting the circumstances in which we found ourselves. It needed an action or force, an energy applied to bring about effective change. By physically altering the environment, the only tangible thing we had control over, we made life better, not perfect, but better. For everything else that we had no authority to manipulate, we utilized the power of prayer. We had to commit. It was all or nothing our backs against the wall with no other resources, there had to be strategies for change, because the alternative was unacceptable.

First, we had to acknowledge we needed help, isolate the problem then take the control of the chaos that was deconstructing our functional family, brought about by sleep deprivation, lack of compartmentalization, social isolation and stress. We learned to recognize warning signs of distress as our bodies were dealing with the onslaught of all of the stimulation, stress and grief. By analyzing our lives to find what we could change, we discovered creative ways of thinking. We took the words of advice from the preschool teachers and turned them into a strategy for goal writing in the IEP process, for building support, for creating a structure towards Kim's future. Working together with professionals, constructing a firm foundation for the continuity of services through a shared vision and philosophy, we were united in the purpose dedicated to supporting an autistic individual to her full potential. Both sides were actively involved in anticipating the next step she would take, building the structure beneath to support her.

As Kim graduated high school and entered college, it seemed that nothing could hold her back. Then it happened. It came on so gradually during the course of two years, at first I didn't notice. Was it another pothole in our autism journey? Was it physical? Mental? Or perhaps it was an accompanying hidden disability? How did we miss such a problem when we had documented her life so carefully?

The point came when I knew something really drastically was wrong. The girl who spoke through her art for almost 2 decades, no longer found the joy or communication in creation. Her hands went silent.

What was about to happen with my daughter would challenge our knowledge from experience of autism and all of the strategies we had developed.

Returning to the tools that had worked in the past, we were able to isolate and identify the elusive problem. Through observations of the patterns in her mind and body along with great cooperation and teamwork with Kim's physician, we adapted strategies and over the course of time, solved the problem. I can stand and say with assurance that those strategies that were used twenty years ago are still as effective today.

John, Marcia, Eileen and Kim

Quick Tips

Strategies that I have used at the advice of Teachers

Autismalize or Normaltistic?

There were some things that Kim did that made me feel uncomfortable at the time. She would spend an unusual amount of time peering, cleaning and examining her toes. No matter what I did, I could not distract her from this obviously fascinating task. It unnerved me that Kim could possibly keep this strange ritual up for years. I tried to discourage her, but when she sensed my disapproval, she began to hide it and became more evasive. She felt a compulsion to examine her toes and sometimes other members of the family as well. I sought out advice from the Early Intervention preschool teacher at the time who suggested I think of what we do typically when we take care of our toes. I drew a blank. The teacher said, "Well, often times, we rub lotions and oils on our feet to make them feel good. Whenever Kim starts with this behavior, bring out some lotion and let her apply it to her feet." It worked beautifully.

This teacher taught me to take a behavior and "normalize it." I refer to it as making something "normaltistic." I have also used an opposite approach when it came to making a typical activity into one that an autistic person would enjoy. That's when I would "autismalize" it by adapting the things that most people would do and make it more autistic friendly.

Consider what the activity is. Open your mind to what typical activity could be adapted or modified in some way to make it a more appropriate activity.

Transition Objects

To coax Kim into being calm while shopping in a store, I would have her focus on an object (stuffed bear, shiny article, or tiny item.) I didn't know it at the time, but what I was doing was giving her a transitional object. She could focus on the article and be able to move from one area to another in the store. As she went to school, she had problems transitioning from one activity in the room to another. By holding something in her hand, she was able to go from free time of playing, to circle/instruction time without tantrum or objection. In my role as a consultant years later, I offered that a particular child could use a transitional object. This idea was soundly shot down. The professionals were very concerned about the fact that if we built in the transitional object into the child's life, that the student would become so dependent on that object, they would still need it years later. It wouldn't be considered socially acceptable to be carrying a teddy bear in High School.

When you think about the objects that we as adults cling to in social situations that are our transitional objects, it is laughable to think that we do so without any objects at all. We have our keys, cell phones, purses, coins... any tiny object. Without realizing it, we all have the objects that help us get from one activity to another. By the way, Kim like everyone else did not need to cling to the objects after she learned the routine and became comfortable with her environment. She looks, acts, and feels like everyone else. If she were an adult that needed a transitional object, we would find something age appropriate (or extremely small) to carry.

Weather related clothing

One of our constant struggles when she was very young was to get her to wear appropriate clothing according to the weather, especially when the seasons changed. She would not change heavy long jean pants to lightweight shorts and when the weather turned cold, change back to pants. After wrestling to dress her, I was out of breath and wondering if it was worth the struggle. A suggestion from Kim's preschool teacher was to cut off her pants until she was wearing shorts in the spring, like somehow they were magically shrinking. Then the opposite process would happen during the fall. I would buy multiple of a couple of pairs of pants to cut off and hem at longer lengths until she were wearing pants. This saved a lot of emotional and physical struggles.

Tactile stimulation from clothing

We allowed Kim the privilege as soon as she came through the door at home, to change into the softest clothing we could find, which was usually a well worn t-shirt, and proper under clothes. Our house was a safety zone where she could be who she was without social judgment. We showed her a series of pictures what was acceptable clothing outside the home, and she could look forward to the relief and release of what she was wearing as soon as she walked through the door. When she changed the clothes, it was like a physical sign or action that told her that it was alright to relax and the tone of that type of environment was translated without words.

Clarification of information

I am of the opinion, "The more information, the better." I could never understand why my typical child seemed to absorb the norms, language, and sequential information from the actions of others- while my child with autism just seemed to have her "slate" wiped clean.

As I talked to Kim's preschool teacher Mary, she told me that I needed to give extremely descriptive and specific terms when speaking to my daughter. Like a visually impaired person is not receiving all the visual information, Kim was not receiving all of the spoken, unspoken signals (inflection and innuendo) in a conversation or directive. Because she did not appear to decode auditory information, we used sign language to add information. We spoke and signed at the same time so that the sign language was in support of verbal information. In her circumstance, spoken words were not her first language; it was like a secondary language. It took a long time for her to respond to a simple question, if at all. She had to turn the language around in her mind to where it made sense, and then formulate and do the reverse process in order to respond. This took a long time.

Many toddlers can respond to a "who," "what," or "why," question. In second grade, when having questions posed on a test, Kim had trouble ascertaining exactly what type of information was being asked, especially if the question was open ended. She had the information, but didn't have the means to discern what information the question was asking for.

If a waitress came to our table and asked, "What would you like to drink?" That would pose a difficulty. My daughter would not know enough to ask about what possibilities there were. My response would either be to cue her to ask for a list of possibilities or to direct her to the menu where the drinks were listed. If time was of the essence such as being on an airplane that has no written menu with the flight attendants precious little time, I would list the possibilities myself. If I were using it as a teaching moment, for Kim to be able to learn to ask for clarification, I would prompt her and model the language that she needed in order to ask the question i.e. "What flavors of drinks do you have?"

When we are out in public and someone asks Kim a question that I can see she clearly doesn't understand, I clarify it by telling her what the intent of the question is, what kind of information the asker is looking for. I narrow down the possibilities of what information she is trying to retrieve

when answering the question by saying, "They want to know *who* gave you
…?" or "*Where* did you find …?" In other words, I step forward to facilitate
the language that is missing. I am the bridge to assist because I know what
part of communication was breaking down. By learning to do this while she
was young (at the suggestion of the Early Intervention teachers), she could
then learn to do this for herself later in life.

Pre-correction

I know that a number of parents of typical children use pre-correction before
going out in public. This is not necessarily a new concept. The family culture
in which I was raised was not to talk of expectations ahead of time, but to
discipline and correct as the situation warranted. So when this suggestion
was brought up to me, it was a foreign concept. This is why I bring this
subject up- because we are all raised differently and exposed to different
ways of thinking.

With autism, this proposal of laying out expectations before going to
an event is very convenient because it fits right into the individuals need
for order.* This can be accomplished by merely talking about the situation
before it occurs. Pictures of drawings or photographs may be used to convey
the arrangement of occasion. By informing the autistic person of the order
of events, the unwritten etiquette, the expectations, they can thereby act
accordingly. Levels of anxiety can be lowered because knowledge keeps
confusion in check. They are reassured by the fact that there are rules and not
rampant chaos. Think of this as a daily briefing or briefing before an event
for the best outcome.

Preparation with changes

An autistic person can be prepared for changes just by informing them that a
change could happen, an alteration in the order of events or changes in persons
attending. I would probably propose that we examine the circumstances
in which a change could occur. In each scenario, I would talk about how
that could make changes, but that the alteration would still make the event
"alright."

Recognizing the Limit of Goodwill

Within Kim, there was a good nature, I call this good nature, "goodwill."
Yes, she was a very frightened wild child, but there was no malice, no anger
from within. However, there was a limit to how long she could spend in
a different environment without having a meltdown (a fit, tantrum, an
emotional upheaval.) This is not to be confused with a child who is tired from

daily activities and requires a nap. It is like when an activity is pleasurable, gets to be too much and behavior gets out of hand. Too much stimulation causes the child's actions to get more wild and frantic until out of control. In Kim's case, this would start with more hyperactivity, louder talking, larger and more exaggerated body movements ending with arching of the back, screeching then totally losing self control.

After we began the Early Intervention program, we started to see the results of our efforts paying off in stretching Kim's attention span, her patience, emotional flexibility, and goodwill. It took an incredible amount of understanding but more importantly, the ability to recognize the signs of when her good will was spent. Once gone, it was impossible to recapture her more calm state. Even a period of rest or sleep at night did not guarantee the restoration of goodwill. She could wake up in the morning (or whenever she actually slept for a period of time) just as unsettled as ever.

It is important that parents and extended family understand not to push an autistic person past their limits because that is when undesirable things start to happen. I will give you an example:

It was the day of my brother's wedding. Kim was doing quite well, but John and I noticed that she was coming to the end of all she could handle. And that end was coming quickly! I was hoping to just quietly leave and call my brother later to congratulate he and his bride and offer apologies for leaving without saying goodbye. We had almost made our way quietly out of the reception hall, when my mother stopped us and told us that it was rude to leave, that we needed to stay to watch the happy couple open the presents. I protested, but obeyed my mother against my better judgment and returned to the festivities, wrangling Kim's flailing body as we went. At first it wasn't too bad. It was like a typical child's squirminess, which turned into a very conspicuously loud, full on wrestle. Finally, Kim grabbed a piece of wrapping paper and raked it across my face, slashing across my eye. I experienced an immediate stinging in my eye. Both eyes were watering so profusely, I could hardly make my way out to the car. John was loading the children in their car seats as I was curled up in pain in the front passenger seat. My mother still chiding me as we drove off. It was 3 days before the pain subsided from the injury to my eye. What was important to my mother was that we hold to the social norms of the wedding, not what was comfortable and manageable for my daughter. She failed to understand or recognize that when Kim was stretched to her limit, her behavior would deteriorate from that point.

The strategy for change here is to recognize when the limit to your child's goodwill has been reached. Pre-correct *your family* before you attend an event. Tell them that you are not being rude, but for everyone's safety and good time, you will leave before your child starts to have problems. Sometimes the rules of etiquette have to be breached, it is not your intention, but when you have an autistic child social niceties sometimes have to be overlooked.

Remember, you are the best judge of your child's behavior. Listen to your heart. You know what is best and don't let anyone pressure you into their agenda.

Index